Clement Moore Lacey Sites

Centralized Administration of Liquor Laws in the American

Commonwealths

Clement Moore Lacey Sites

Centralized Administration of Liquor Laws in the American Commonwealths

ISBN/EAN: 9783337233228

Printed in Europe, USA, Canada, Australia, Japan

Cover: Foto ©Suzi / pixelio.de

More available books at **www.hansebooks.com**

CENTRALIZED ADMINISTRATION OF LIQUOR LAWS

IN THE

AMERICAN COMMONWEALTHS

BY

CLEMENT MOORE LACEY SITES, LL.B., A.M.

Sometime Fellow in Constitutional Law

SUBMITTED IN PARTIAL FULFILMENT OF THE REQUIREMENTS
FOR THE DEGREE OF DOCTOR OF PHILOSOPHY
IN THE
FACULTY OF POLITICAL SCIENCE
COLUMBIA UNIVERSITY

New York
1899

PREFACE

IN quest of facts I have had to presume upon the courtesy of officials and private persons in many parts of the country. I owe them much, not only for facts, but for clews that led to facts. While statutes, decisions and official reports furnish most of the data, valuable suggestions have also been derived from such studies of liquor legislation as "The Liquor Problem in its Legislative Aspects," published by the Committee of Fifty; "Liquor Legislation in the United States," by E. L. Fanshawe; "Prohibition," by E. J. Wheeler, and numerous current publications.

COLUMBIA UNIVERSITY, *April, 1899.*

TABLE OF CONTENTS

INTRODUCTION

CHAPTER I

EXCISE REVENUE ADMINISTRATION

I. *Development*

II. *Current Forms*

CHAPTER II

RESTRICTIVE LICENSE ADMINISTRATION

I. *Development*

II. *Current Forms*

CHAPTER III

Repressive Police Administration

CHAPTER IV

COMMERCIAL ADMINISTRATION

I. *Development*

II. *Current Form*

CONCLUSION

PRESENT TENDENCIES IN LIQUOR LEGISLATION

INTRODUCTION

In the regulation of the liquor traffic the several commonwealths of the United States have followed widely variant policies. All plans of regulation are based, however, upon the broad powers of taxation and police. The several commonwealths, being practically supreme in the exercise of these powers upon subjects of local concern, regulate the traffic within their borders by general laws; or at least it is regulated under the authority of laws enacted by the central legislature of each commonwealth.

We hear much of characteristic plans of regulation of the liquor traffic, but comparatively little of characteristic systems of administration. The reason is that few commonwealths have any real system. The liquor laws are administered incoherently. As we have no national consensus in plans of regulation, so we have, in most instances, no commonwealth consensus in standards of administration. The legislature may frame a plan of administration, prescribing the duties of local officers; but each community practically determines for itself how the law shall be enforced. Where the local consensus is against enforcement, the law generally proves a dead letter; and unless the restrictions imposed by the law are toned down to accord with local ideals, some special measures must be taken to secure enforcement.

Many expedients have been adopted to remedy the defect. Legislative control has been strengthened through a multitude of statutory details which have prescribed official duties with great precision and added new penal sanctions. The failure of the general law in particular localities has been met with special legislation. Judicial control has been extended, in order to subject the local administration more effectually to the supervision of the courts. Sometimes, but less generally, local officers have been placed under the direct control of the central administration.

Administrative control may be, in general, of two kinds. First, local officers may be subjected to the supervision and the more or less effective direction of a central administrative head; or, secondly, the central administration may be extended downward, in the persons of its own appointees, to the immediate performance of the acts which would otherwise devolve upon local officers. The first kind is properly termed central administrative control; the second, centralized administration. The two shade off into each other; in general discussion, either term may be used to cover both ideas. The administrative control with which this inquiry is concerned is that exercised by the central executive officers of the commonwealth. It is a departure from the general American policy of decentralized administration.

The sort of administrative activity required in the enforcement of a particular liquor law depends, of course, upon the plan of regulation which the law provides. The various plans of regulation may be roughly classified according to the dominant aspect in which they regard the liquor traffic. It has been treated: (1) as an open traffic to be carried on by private enterprise for public accommodation, subject simply to taxation and to reasonable safeguards; (2) as a necessary but dangerous business, to be limited to approved persons and approved places, and, like the manufacture of explosives, to be surrounded with special safeguards; (3) as a criminal enterprise, to be suppressed, like highway robbery; and (4) as a subject of legal monopoly, which may be assumed by the government itself, primarily for police

regulation, secondarily for revenue. The spheres of administration that correspond to these theories of legislation may
be broadly distinguished as Revenue, License, Police and
Commercial. The term " license " is here employed with
special regard to the restrictions which it connotes and with
no special regard to revenue. The term " police " is employed, for convenience, in its common signification, to mean
the province of the administration in the preservation of the
peace and the apprehension of law-breakers, not "the
police power " in the broad sense.

The administrative spheres, like the legislative theories,
intersect and overlap. Moreover, a fifth sphere of administrative activity is partly involved in each of the others,
namely, the instituting and maintaining of judicial proceedings. In so far as centralized administration obtains, these
five spheres of activity afford a convenient scheme for its
classification. In each of these spheres there have been, in
recent years, such marked developments of centralized administration as to give this phase of the liquor problem a
peculiar present interest. It is the object of this essay to
study these developments.

It is not proposed to catalogue the instances of central
control. To do this would involve not only the legislative
history of all the commonwealths, but all the changes of
current politics. It is impossible even to give assurance of
accuracy in the use of the tenses. Centralized systems in
operation a year ago have since been abolished, some by
legislative acts and some through judicial decisions. Others
have risen in the interval. The aim is to present the characteristic features of a period or of a class. No attempt is
made, in most instances, to present specific results of centralization. Valuable intensive studies of particular systems
have been made and are making, giving statistical details.
The aim here is to present administrative forms and to

consider their relations to particular regulative plans in the light of the principles of political science.   In each chapter, therefore, so far as the topic permits, the development of centralization will first be noticed, current forms will then be described, together with as full an account as is practicable of their actual operation, and finally the theory upon which they rest will be discussed.   In the conclusion an attempt will be made to indicate certain tendencies, closely connected with administrative problems, in the liquor legislation of the day.

consider their relations to particular regulative plans in the light of the principles of political science. In each chapter, therefore, so far as the topic permits, the development of centralization will first be noticed, current forms will then be described, together with as full an account as is practicable of their actual operation, and finally the theory upon which they rest will be discussed. In the conclusion an attempt will be made to indicate certain tendencies, closely connected with administrative problems, in the liquor legislation of the day.

CHAPTER I

EXCISE REVENUE ADMINISTRATION

I. *Development*

THE term "excise" has been particularly connected in English law with the special tax on liquors. An excise on ale, beer, cider and perry was levied by Parliament in 1643. "This was the first time that ever the name of payment of excise was heard of or practised in England."[1] An interesting side light upon its administration is afforded in Johnson's definition of excise in 1755: "A hateful tax levied upon commodities, and adjudged not by the common judges of property, but wretches hired by those to whom excise is paid." In the American colonies the term was generally used to signify a tax on liquors. Jefferson wrote in 1789: "In Massachusetts they have perverted the word excise to mean a tax on all liquors, whether paid in the moment of importation or at a later moment, and on nothing else." Massachusetts was not peculiar in this respect. The term seems to have been used in the same sense in a New Hampshire act of the 5th year of George II, "for granting unto his Majesty an excise on several liquors," which provided for the payment of a quarterly excise by "tavern keepers, innholders and retailers," to an appointed receiver.[2] In some of the colonies and early commonwealths, the excise was a temporary expedient for emergency revenue. Thus the

---

[1] Clarendon, *History of the Rebellion*, IV, 418 (Oxford, 1826).

[2] *Laws of the Province of New Hampshire* (1759).

Virginia laws of the Revolutionary period show that the legislature frequently resorted to a tax of a few pounds on ordinaries. Massachusetts was peculiar in that her license laws for many years following the Revolution made no mention of special fees or taxes, the stress of legislation being laid upon fines and penalties. The license law of 1787 requires, however, that the bond given by the licensee shall be liable for any excise duty that may be levied.[1] In 1831 it was provided that there should be paid for the license "an excise of $5" for the sale of "strong liquors" and one of $1 for the sale of wines and malt liquors;[2] but this excise disappeared in the elaborate license law of the following year.[3] In one colony the excise on liquors was persistently employed as a means of revenue, and most of its liquor legislation as a commonwealth has had revenue as a basis. This was New York. Its machinery for the collection of the excise in colonial times showed less central administrative control than could be found in some of the other colonies; but the development of its administrative system in this field illustrates colonial methods of collection, and is instructive in view of the highly specialized and centralized system which the commonwealth has recently established. Central administrative control of the liquor revenue in colonial times through the formal centralizing of license administration will be noticed in the next chapter.

The excise in early New York was levied upon the retail trade only and was chiefly collected through the method of farming. Until 1709 its collection was irregular. In that year the provincial assembly granted the excise on liquors to the Queen, and local authorities were empowered to "lett to Farme the said Excise," making returns quarterly

---

[1] *Act of* Feb. 28, 1787.   [2] *Act of* Mar. 19, 1831.
[3] *Act of* Mar. 24, 1832.

to the treasurer of the colony.[1]   This excise-levy was distinct from the licensing of "innkeepers and ordinaryes,"
which was generally committed to the justices in the sessions in the colony at large [2] and to the centrally appointed
mayor in New York city and Albany.[3]   The general excise
was fixed at 12*d*. per gallon on "strong liquors" and 6*s*. per
barrel on "beer and syder," afterward expressed as one-
eighth of an ounce and three-quarters of an ounce of plate,
respectively." [4]

The irregularities of collection through local officials led
the legislature to assume a direct control of the administration of the excise.   In 1714 there was passed "An act for
appointing commissioners to let to farm the excise throughout this colony."   Commissioners were named, in the act, for
the several counties, with discretion to conduct the farming
of the excise "for the better advancement of the duty and
excise," which they were to receive, and, in case of de-
linquency, to sue for.   The commissioners were required to
account to the treasurer of the colony, under bond, and
were allowed, as compensation, a commission on their
receipts, varying, in different counties, from seven and one-
half to ten per cent.[5]

Centralized though it was, as compared with what had
gone before, this system had none of the elements of central
administrative control.   It might easily have developed into
such a system.   So far as the administration was centralized
it was a sort of legislative administration.   The exercise by
the legislature of the administrative function of appointment
was one of the incidents in the dramatic contest between
representative government and royal prerogative which en-
livens the history of provincial New York.[6]   So jealous was

---

[1] *Act of* June 8, 1709.

[2] *The Dongan Charters* (1686).

[5] *Act of* Sept. 4, 1714.

[3] *The Duke of York's Laws* (1665).

[4] *Act of* Oct. 15, 1713.

[6] *Cf., e.g., N. Y. Colonial Documents*, V, 82.

the Assembly of the power of appointment that it was provided that in case any of the commissioners named " Dye, Deny or Refuse to serve," the vacancy should be filled *ad interim* by the local authorities, not by the governor.[1] The discretionary powers of the commissioners, coupled with their freedom from efficient control, seem to have produced unsatisfactory results. During the three years of the continuance of this system, we find it variously amended; the commissioners being urged to " the greater increase of the said excise" and being made liable to a fine of £50 for retailing on their own account.[2]

The system of farming the excise reached its highest limit in the Act of Nov. 9, 1717, whereby the legislature contracted directly with two men, Francis Harrison and Gilbert Livingstone, as " Farmers General" of the excise, for a lump sum of 3750 ounces of plate yearly. Strictly speaking, excise administration as a function of government was, by this act, eliminated. Beginning with the letting of the excise farm by the local officials under general legislative supervision, the governmental functions in excise administration had been successively narrowed to particular officials and, finally, to the legislature itself. At the same time, and *pari passu*, what might be called the subgovernmental functions of excise administration had advanced in importance. The farmers of the excise occupied the place of official collectors. The farmers-general under the Act of 1717, although standing in contractual and not in official relations to the government, enjoyed such wide powers that their functions may be considered as *quasi*-administrative; and the system now instituted may be regarded as a highly centralized exercise of governmental powers with the substitution, at the head of the system, of the motive of private gain for that of official duty.

[1] *Ibid.*   [2] *Act of* Sept. 1, 1716.

These farmers-general were, by the terms of the act of 1717, " authorized and empowered, by themselves, their agents, deputies or assigns, to collect and receive the said duty of excise, given and granted by the act before mentioned, and all the fines, penalties and forfeitures that shall arise or become due by virtue of the said act or by virtue of this or any other act * * *." They might sublet or assign their contract at will, saving always the liability of their sureties to the provincial government. All retailers were required to come to the farmers, " give a true and just account of all the said liquors received by them " and make payment of the excise; in default whereof they " shall forfeit all such liquors and three times the value thereof," recovery to be had through legal procedure, with commitment to the " common gaol " until payment made. The right of search is conferred, the farmers being authorized, broadly, to enter for the purpose of gauging and taking account of the stock of retailers, obstruction being made liable to a fine of £10. Finally, the powers of the farmers are crowned with the authority to " compound, compromise and agree with any the persons offending, contrary to the meaning of this act, and to remit all or any part of the penalties and forfeitures as they shall think fit." In addition to the payment of the stipulated sum annually to the treasurer of the colony, the farmers-general were required only to render to the governor, before the expiration of the five-year term, " a just and true account," showing the sums received by them annually, and from whom received. This final account was never rendered. Owing to the derangement of trade resulting from the war with Spain, " which has affected the publique houses or persons retailing strong liquors,"¹ the plan failed before the term was half run, and the commissioner system was resumed.² The plan of contracting directly with individuals

---

¹ *Act of* July 27, 1721.   ² *Act of* Nov. 19, 1720.

as farmers of the excise in the several counties was next tried, and prevailed for several years, the farmers being named usually by the legislature.

In 1753, the farming policy, which had assumed such various administrative forms, was abandoned. In place of the sum formerly paid by the farmer of excise to the government, the excise tax was assessed proportionally among the several counties, to be sub-assessed among the several retailers—in most of the counties by county commissioners named in the act.[1] Instead of profits to contract-farmers and commissions to official auctioneers, a fixed amount was allowed the several commissioners, to be collected as a fee, in addition to the tax. The provincial government, through its own administrative officers, thus finally came in contact with the tax-payer. At the top of the system was the legislature, assuming administrative functions. The substitution of an executive control in the appointment and supervision of the commissioners would have made it a consistent system of administrative centralization. That stage of development was not reached during the colonial period; and when a specially centralized excise administration under executive control was instituted after the Revolution, for certain cities, it was involved with license functions. In the meantime the excise revenues had been remitted to local uses. The term "excise" persisted, even in license laws; and it has assumed again its peculiar significance, within recent years, in connection with centralized administration.[2]

II. *Current Forms*

The transition from historic forms of excise administration to current forms is accentuated by two facts of modern

[1] *Act of* Dec. 12, 1753.

[2] For a comprehensive outline of excise development in New York, see J. A. Fairlie's *Centralization of Administration in New York State.*

legislative policy which, in turn, arise from changed conditions of social life. First, the liquor traffic is generally taxed, in the several commonwealths, not primarily for the raising of revenue but peculiarly for purposes of regulation. Secondly, most of the retail trade has moved away from the " grocery " on the one hand and the " tavern " on the other, and has become a " bar-room " traffic ; the " saloon," rather than the " store," is the source of excise revenue. The change is reflected in the general substitution of " license " laws for " excise " laws. Nevertheless, the taxation of the traffic is conducted, in some commonwealths, on a revenue basis. The cases in which revenue considerations may be regarded as shaping the excise policy fall into two classes, (1) the taxation of the liquor traffic as a particular item in a general system of business or privilege taxes ; and (2) the exaction of a special tax, usually rather high, upon the traffic, without the requirement of license as a condition precedent to engaging in it. In either class of cases regulation may be one of the objects of the impost ; in the second class it is likely to be a most important object ; but in both, the financial considerations give shape to the administrative organization.

Several of the southern commonwealths belong to the first class ; in some of these, although the term " license " is used, it imports practically no restrictive administration. Where a great variety of occupations are taxed for the benefit of the commonwealth under a general license revenue law, its application is so extensive that it is not likely to be very intensive. For the same reason no very marked centralization is to be expected in the revenue administration of such systems. Some cases belonging to the second class, too, show no administrative control worthy of mention, as, for instance, Ohio, whose simple liquor tax, imposed upon the traffic wherever found, follows the course of general revenue through the hands of county officers. It is evident, however, that when the liquor excise is specialized, it lends itself readily to centralization of revenue administration.

1. CENTRAL CONTROL OF EXCISE AS A BRANCH OF GENERAL REVENUE

(1) *Central Supervision of Local Collectors*

Administrative supervision of the collection of the commonwealth revenues may be exercised by the ordinary fiscal officers of the commonwealth or through offices created specially for the purpose. In its lowest stage such authority amounts to little more than the right to examine books, preliminary to bringing suit. In Tennessee, where liquor licenses are issued by the county clerk to all applicants who fulfil certain prescribed conditions, as a part of a general system of business licenses, payment of a definite tax for commonwealth purposes is exacted; and the Comptroller of the Treasury is authorized to employ special agents whom he may send into any and all counties to investigate the books of local collectors, and, in case of delinquencies, to bring suit.[1] In Alabama, where licenses are issued and the commonwealth tax received by the Probate Judge, regular reports to the Auditor and regular remittances to the Treasurer are required. In default of such returns within ten days after they are due, the Auditor may report the facts to the Governor, who may cite the judge to show cause, failing in which the judge is subject to impeachment proceedings to be instituted by the executive before the Supreme Court. Here the enforcement of all revenue laws is placed under the supervision of the Auditor, who directs assessors and collectors generally in their duties and furnishes uniform blanks for their use.[2]

Somewhat more specialized is the revenue supervision

[1] *Laws of* 1879, ch. 218, *as amended,* 1891.

[2] *Acts of* Dec. 12, 1884; Dec. 11, 1886.

provided in Mississippi, where a " State Revenue Agent,"
elected by the people, is empowered to investigate delinquencies of local officers in matters of commonwealth
revenue and to enforce payment, taking for compensation a
commission of 20 per cent.[1]   Out of this allowance he must
pay all his expenses, including the employment of " a sufficient number of deputies."   Inasmuch as a tax of $1200 is
exacted, for the use of the commonwealth, upon every
licensed dramshop in cities, in addition to the local license
charge,[2] the Revenue Agent is likely to be much concerned
with the liquor excise, despite the wide prevalence of local
prohibition.

In Texas the officer known as the " State Revenue Agent"
is endowed with still more definite functions looking toward
administrative control.[3]   He has less official independence
than the officer similarly entitled in Mississippi, and correspondingly adds the important element of unity to the
executive control of revenue administration.   He is appointed by the Governor, " who may, whenever in his judgment the public service demands it," institute investigations
of the books and accounts of all financial officers, and may
cause the " State Revenue Agent " to perform such duties
" in the interest of the public revenues as the Governor may
direct."   Summary administrative jurisdiction is wanting,
the Governor being limited in ultimate remedies to civil and
criminal proceedings based upon the reports of the " State
Revenue Agent."   This officer, however, exercises an indirect coërcive influence over the local administration through
the requirement of regular reports, especially in the matter
of excise.   A specific tax of $300 being exacted by the
commonwealth upon every dramshop, the county clerk is

---

[1] *Code* (1892), ch. 126.   *Laws of* 1894, ch. 34.

[2] *Code* (1892), ch. 37.

[3] *Texas Revised Statutes* (1895), Arts 5058–60.

required to forward a monthly statement of applications, and the local tax-collector a monthly statement of liquor taxes paid, to the office of the revenue agent.

(2) *Direct Collection of Tax by the Commonwealth.*

Immediate collection of taxes by commonwealth officers is rare. In northern cities liquor license charges are sometimes collected by centrally appointed officers when such officers also discharge license functions. In nearly all cases where central revenue is involved the entire charge is collected by one officer or set of officers. An instance of division of administration, extending however only to the metropolitan district, is found in Louisiana. The commonwealth, as is usual in the south, imposes an elaborate system of business taxes, including a tax upon the sale of liquors which is graduated according to the amount of gross receipts. In the parish of Orleans, comprising the city of New Orleans, these taxes are collected by collectors appointed by the Governor.[1] The municipality may regulate the traffic at will, impose additional taxation or license-charges for its own use and collect them through its own agents. Throughout the other parishes, commonwealth taxes are collected by the sheriffs, who are held to account under penalties to be recovered by judicial process. An inchoate central control may be found in the provision that "the Governor shall designate for each parish an attorney at law," to aid the collector, to be paid by commissions, and to be removable in the pleasure of the Governor.[2]

2. SPECIALIZED EXCISE ADMINISTRATION.

The Liquor Tax Law of New York[3] affords the most complete example of centralized excise administration "for

[1] *Laws of* 1888, ch. 85.   [2] *Act of* July 9, 1890.

[3] *Laws of* 1896, ch. 112; 1897, ch. 312; 1898, ch. 167. References are to the law as amended in 1898.

revenue only." It employs both the principal plans of centralization, viz., direct administration by centrally appointed officers, and summary powers of discipline over local officers. The law cannot pretend to the simplicity of a mere act of taxation, for it abounds in restrictions and precepts; but its restrictions, so far as they involve conditions precedent, are conclusively defined by the legislature, leaving nothing to administrative discretion; and its precepts, so far as they relate to the preservation of peace and order, are committed to the care of the local police. There is left the well-defined field of revenue administration, limited almost exclusively to ministerial functions. This branch of administration is centralized and forms the characteristic administrative feature of the law.

The payment of a tax, graduated according to the population of the place and the character of the traffic, is one of the conditions precedent to engaging in the traffic. The tax is received by the county treasurer, except in the counties containing the city of Buffalo, the former cities of New York and Brooklyn, and Staten Island, respectively. In these it is received by a special deputy commissioner of excise appointed for each of these counties by the "State Commissioner of Excise."[1] County treasurers receiving the liquor tax are required to pay over the share due the commonwealth (one-third of the receipts), to the commonwealth treasurer within ten days after receipt, and to render complete accounts to the commissioner of excise, in form prescribed by him, as often as he shall direct.[2] Any county treasurer derelict in the duties enjoined by this act is subject to removal from office in the discretion of the governor, "after hearing and determination thereon and decision that such neglect or refusal has occurred."[3]

[1] *Ibid.,* § 9.　　　　　　　　　　　[2] *Ibid.,* §§ 13, 15.

[3] *Ibid.,* § 38.

Similar accounting is required of the special deputy commissioners. Their tenure being by appointment of the commissioner and their term being in his pleasure, they are under efficient administrative control from the head of the system.

The commissioner of excise is appointed by the governor with the concurrence of the senate for a five-year term,[1] and is only removable, like other heads of departments, by the same authority.[2] In him, therefore, administrative control centers. Although the ultimate administrative control over certain county officers is reserved to the governor, various auxiliary lines of control place the actual revenue administration almost completely in the hands of the commissioner. In addition to the appointment of the deputy commissioners and of the clerical force in his own and his deputies' offices these lines of control are as follows:

(1) Sixty special agents, appointed by the commissioner and removable in his pleasure, are given wide powers to " investigate all matters relating to the collection of liquor taxes and penalties under this act, and in relation to the compliance with law by persons engaged in the traffic in liquors."[3] Through these officials the department undertakes to detect perjuries committed in obtaining liquor tax certificates and to discover cases of trafficking in liquors without payment of the prescribed tax, concurrently with the local police.

(2) Besides securing legal assistance in the ordinary work of the department the commissioner may freely appoint attorneys to act independently of local prosecuting officers in any " proceeding brought under the provisions of this act."[4] At the same time all district attorneys are held to a

[1] *Ibid.*, § 6.

[2] *The Public Officers Law, Gen. Laws* (1896), ch. 7.

[3] *Liquor Tax Law*, § 10.   [4] *Ibid.*

vigorous prosecution of offenders, under the summary sanction of removal by the governor as in the case of delinquent county treasurers.[1] In all cases of offenses of such a nature as to infringe the revenue, such as trafficking in liquors without payment of tax, or any breach of the conditions of a bond, the commissioner of excise may sue for the penalty without waiting for action by local prosecuting officers.[2] Penalties thus recovered accrue, undivided, to the central treasury.

(3) Fines and penalties imposed by any court under the provisions of this act are to be entered as judgments in favor of the commissioner of excise, and paid over to the deputy commissioner or county treasurer to be distributed in the same manner as the liquor tax.[3] " The court or officer imposing the sentence, or the clerk of the court if there be a clerk," is required immediately to send to the commissioner a transcript of such judgment and to notify him of the payment thereof when made.[4] County clerks are required to make monthly reports to the commissioner of excise, giving full details of all judicial proceedings in which the commissioner is concerned.[5] The commissioner may call upon the county clerk for complete certified copies of the official papers in any case, and the clerk's fees for such services are made a legal charge against the county. Any magistrate, moreover, before whom a person charged with violation of the liquor tax law shall be brought for preliminary hearing, shall, if the person be held, immediately notify the commissioner of excise, giving all essential facts, including names of witnesses.[6] Finally, all liquor tax certificates forfeited in consequence of convictions for violation of

[1] *Ibid.*, § 38.
[2] *Ibid.*, §§ 18, 42.   (See also Chapter V.)
[3] *Ibid.*, § 36.   [4] *Ibid.*
[5] *Ibid.*   [6] *Ibid.*, § 35.

the law must be forwarded through the deputy commissioner or county treasurer to the commissioner, for cancellation; and rebates on surrendered certificates can be paid only upon his order.[1]

In some of these lines of centralization the commissioner has only a supervisory authority. In general he has no summary powers of discipline over local officers. He has peculiar powers in invoking judicial control, however, which will be considered hereafter.[2]

In several minor particulars the position of the commissioner as the controlling head of an elaborate administrative system is emphasized. He provides uniform books of record and liquor tax certificates;[3] he receives, direct, the tax imposed upon common carriers who traffic in liquors;[4] and he alone may, by a special order, authorize the entry and inspection of the club-houses of clubs which "traffic in liquors solely with the members thereof."[5] In order to determine the population class to which any city or village belongs, in case of "doubts as to the number of the population as affecting the amount of the excise tax," the commissioner may make his own enumeration, first establishing a boundary line where such line has not been determined.[6]

The results of centralized administration in New York must be considered in connection with the purpose of the law. This purpose was two-fold: (1) to regulate the traffic without leaving to administrative officers the duty of discrimination among would-be traffickers;[7] (2) to increase

---

[1] *Ibid.*, § 25.

[2] See Chapter V.

[3] *Liquor Tax Law*, § 15.

[4] *Ibid.*, § 13.

[5] *Ibid.*, § 37.

[6] *Ibid.*, § 11, subd. 4.

[7] See article, "*The Raines Liquor Tax Law*," by Senator John Raines, *N. A. Review*, Apr., 1896.

the public revenue from the traffic. The police regulations imposed by the law do not differ essentially from those of recently preceding laws; but the sudden withdrawal from local officers of both license and revenue functions led to a disposition on the part of officers in some populous localities to forbear the execution of the repressive functions which were distinctly reserved to them. At the same time the high tax imposed stimulated the natural instinct of dealers to increase their receipts, by evasions, such as the establishment of pretended clubs[1] and hotels, and also by direct violations of the law, not only through sales without certificate but through sales at forbidden hours. The heavy penalties prescribed conspired to defeat the ends of the statute through the willingness of local courts and juries to accept any technical defense. These circumstances contributed to a degree of odium with which many good citizens regarded the new enactment. In none of these conditions, however, was the theory of centralized administration directly involved.

The financial showing of the liquor tax law is, to a large extent, independent of the centralized character of its revenue administration. The mere comparison of figures between the old system and the new would be a poor indication of the efficiency of central control. The expense attending the local collection of license fees from 33,437 licensees in 1895–6 was $252,782.77; the expense of collecting the excise tax on 24,116 drinking places in 1897–8 was $324,595.25. The quadrupling of the impost, while it increases the difficulty of repressing evasions, adds but a small absolute amount to the ordinary costs of collection. The fact, therefore, that the net revenue for the former year was $2,919,593.81, and for the latter year $11,500,133.90, is not a matter of great administrative significance.[2]

---

[1] See, *e. g., In re* Lyman, 50 *N. Y. Supp.*, 898.

[2] *Reports of State Commissioner of Excise*, 1897-8-9.

While neither the deficiencies of police enforcement nor the increase of revenue can strictly be ascribed to the centralized administrative system, this system is part of a consistent plan whose moral effects must be judged with some breadth of view. The revenue administrative system, as the central element in the plan, dominates and tends to set the standard for all the other administrative elements. A uniform business management, under effective control, gives to the local police administration at least an assured basis for supplementary vigilance, besides the stimulus of responsibility for the independent working out of a uniform plan of regulation. If we grant the expediency of the arrogation of all restrictive discretion to the legislative authority, with the consequent relegating of the traffic to the primary control of economic laws, then the natural sequel is the administration of such tax as may be imposed upon the traffic on the principles most conducive to business efficiency. The simple functions incident to the collection of a specific tax are less likely to incur the private citizen's resentment of governmental interference than the police activities of government. They admit, therefore, of a correspondingly higher degree of centralized administration without the probability of its being overthrown by popular dissatisfaction. The impetus of efficiency which may thus be developed in the positive functions of financial administration tends to induce a subsidiary activity in the repressive functions of local administration. The commissioner of excise reports, in 1899: "In very many sections of the state, where a year ago public officials would neither recognize nor do their duty with reference to excise affairs, at present what appears to be a good-faith effort for the law's enforcement is being made."[1]

The powers of financial control vested in the commissioner

[1] P. 38.

have been effectively exercised. The accounts of special deputy commissioners and county treasurers are regularly checked up at the central office. Errors are thus corrected and uniformity secured. Every treasurer's office was visited "one or more times during the year, and in many instances visits had to be made to the supervisors of towns and fiscal officers of cities."[1] Persistent effort during the three years since the centralized system was inaugurated has secured the efficient coöperation of these local officers. "All moneys due the state at the expiration of the fiscal year from delinquent county treasurers have been collected, and where liquor taxes collected and due towns and cities have been unlawfully held back the matter has been followed up and payment to the local fiscal officer exacted."[2]

The excise department insists upon the strictly fiscal character of its functions, declining to assume the responsibility of exercising discretion in the issue of the certificate which evidences the right to traffic. The commissioner says:

From its organization, the Department has maintained that the applicant for a liquor tax certificate must assume the responsibility of his own statements and furnish the facts which entitle him to a certificate; that if he conforms to the act in making the requisite statements, furnishes all the consents required, files a bond which is correct in form, with the sufficient sureties, and pays the tax, then the certificate-issuing officer 'shall at once issue a certificate,' as specifically provided in the act.[3]

It being manifestly impracticable for the department, with but half a hundred active agents, to verify the allegations of the applicants before granting certificates, its activities in this respect are remedial instead of preventive. Of the violations of law reported by the special agents in the year 1897–8, two hundred and eighty-one were deemed of suffi-

[1] *Report*, 1899, p. 25–6.   [2] *Ibid.*
[3] *Report*, 1899, p. 18.

cient importance by the department to be referred to the several district attorneys for criminal prosecution.[1] During the same year the department brought 177 civil actions against parties to enforce payment of excise taxes, for the revocation of certificates improperly obtained, etc.[2] In a majority of these cases special attorneys were employed, to represent the commissioner. The duties of the special agents, therefore, are closely analogous to those of the United States internal revenue agents. They constitute a revenue constabulary, the active arm of the prosecuting authority in enforcing the penal sanctions of a revenue measure. Incidentally they contribute to the police enforcement of the law by local officers; but revenue administration is kept so distinct from the functions of peace officers that the New York "special agent" system has already reached a degree of specialization which makes it historically more fit to survive than any centralized police constabulary.

III. *Theory.*

The conditions conducive to centralized administration of excise may be described in one word—definiteness. Taxation of the traffic wherever found leads more readily to central control of revenue administration than a license policy, because the operation of economic law is more uniform than the exercise of official discretion. A settled policy as to the amount of the tax and its distribution contributes to the same end. The most potent of all causes of efficiency and stability in centralized administration is definiteness in the subject matter with which the administration deals. Let it be concerned solely with the excise on liquors and specifically with the revenue arising therefrom,

[1] *Report*, 1899, p. 24.

[2] *Ibid.* See, for details as to such proceedings, Chapter V.

and an executive department may be easily and highly centralized. Revenue administration being peculiarly a matter of business as distinguished from police administration, which depends largely upon¸sentiment, it lends itself readily to the application of business methods in respect to organization and concentration of authority.

In so far as taxation is resorted to as a means of regulating the traffic, the more efficient the ·revenue administration the more effective will be the restraint imposed. The separation of revenue administration from police administration may afford a pretext for the ₍neglect of police enforcement on a plea of divided responsibility; but a division of responsibility, when it is effectually made, should be conducive to increased efficiency in both parts. As between revenue and police administration, if one is to be centralized and one localized, the police functions should be left to the local control of every community which is able and willing to discharge them. The centralizing of revenue is the more natural, the more effectual and the more likely, by setting an example of efficiency, to elevate the general tone of excise administration.

CHAPTER II

I. *Development*

DISCRIMINATION among persons in privileges of trade may be made for purposes of revenue or for purposes of regulation. When made for purposes of regulation it is an exercise of the police power in the broadest sense. The actual exercise of this power by an administrative authority remote from the community affected is usually attended with local dissatisfaction in a degree corresponding to the interest of the people in the restricted traffic. The old English practice of decentralized administration re-appeared or was perpetuated in the New England town, where licenses were usually granted on recommendation of the selectmen, and in the southern county, where they were granted by the justices in quarter sessions. Centralization in this branch of administration had no marked development in the United States until the peculiar conditions of politics in the larger cities made it an expedient either of good government or of partisan advantage. A formal central control, with little actual efficacy, is frequently found, however, in colonial times.

A good example of the purely formal centralization of licensing authority in the early period is presented in Pennsylvania. An act of the provincial assembly passed in 1710 provides as follows:

For preventing disorders and the mischiefs that may arise from multiplicity of public houses of entertainment, *Be it enacted,* That

36   [256

no person or persons whatsoever within this province shall hereafter
have or keep any public inn, tavern, ale-house, tippling house or
dramshop, victualling house or public house of entertainment, in any
county of this province or in the city of Philadelphia, unless such
person or persons shall first be recommended by the Justices in the
respective county courts, and the said city, in their Quarter Sessions
or Court of Record for the said counties and cities respectively, to
the Lieutenant-Governor for the time being for his license for so
doing, under the penalty of five pounds.[1]

This formal centralization continued after the Revolution,
the commonwealth governor succeeding the colonial lieutenant-governor as the nominal grantor of the license.   In 1794
we find clerks of quarter sessions authorized to procure
licenses, in blank, from the secretary of the commonwealth
to be issued by the county treasurer to persons approved by
the justices.[2]   In 1807, signing by the secretary of the commonwealth was substituted for signing by the governor[3] and
in 1815 all provisions for signing of licenses by central
officers were repealed.[4]   The gradual abandonment of the
formality emphasizes the formal character of the control.

Delaware illustrates a similar phase of formal centralization.   Permission to sell strong drinks was obtained, in the
colonial period, " by petition and recommendation from the
justices of the court of quarter sessions, to his honor the
governor for the time being, for a license for keeping the
same." [5]   In this case the old form still lingers, the general
code providing for licenses to be granted by the courts of
general sessions, but signed and sealed by the governor
and the secretary of state.[6]   In Pennsylvania the disappear-
ance of the central license formality was followed in time by

[1] *Laws of* 1710 (1 *Sm. L.* 73).   [2] *Laws,* (1794); ch. 1752. .

[3] Ch. 2858.   [4] Ch. 4963 (6 *Sm. L.* 265).

[5] 13 *Geo. II.*   [6] *R. S.,* 1893, ch. 531.

the relinquishment of the license revenues to local treasuries. In Delaware, where the form of centralization persists, fees and penalties under the general law accrue to the use of the commonwealth.[3]

These instances illustrate a plan of express but nominal centralization of license authority where the actual authority was exercised by judicial officers. Where the licensing power was exercised in name as well as in fact by the justices of the peace it might be supposed that the central executive could still exert an efficient control through the power of appointment of justices. In its practical effect upon license 'functions, however, this control was of slight importance. The element of definiteness was wanting. License administration was a minor incident in the functions of the justice. Moreover, the traditions of the office were directly opposed to the principle of central administrative control. The constant tendency of the office was toward responsibility to the people instead of to the central administration.

Nevertheless it is worthy of note that the justice and the sheriff, as formal representatives of the central fountain of authority, carried that authority into the domain not only of license but of penal administration. In so far as the magistrate was empowered to direct the local constables, as he might in rural districts, he was not only license commissioner but police commissioner. The office thus foreshadowed, in a way, the union of restrictive and repressive functions which is frequently found in the police board of a modern city.

Although administrative functions proper were associated with judicial functions in the justice, there were evidences of a tendency to withdraw license administration from the justice when license was involved to any considerable extent

[3] *R. S.*, 1893, ch. 531.

with revenue. In South Carolina, for instance, as early as 1695, the license fee for sale of liquors generally was £5. In 1709 we find the fee regarded as a perquisite of the Governor, and in 1711 licenses were granted by a board of three commissioners,[1] although an act of the same year, for the regulating of " Taverns and Punch Houses," provides that any two justices of the peace may enforce the laws of England against disorder therein.[2] A period of judicial administration began in 1741, but in 1751 the Governor was empowered to limit the licenses granted;[3] and at the close of the century liquor licenses were granted by and in the discretion of the " Commissioners of Roads, in their respective districts and parishes." [4]

The assumption of a formal central control of license as a mere check on revenue returns re-appeared later in Maryland. At the time of the Revolution, licenses were granted by the county courts, in their discretion, at fixed fees which accrued to the central treasury.[5] In 1828, it having been found difficult to secure definite accounting by local collectors, discretion was withdrawn and " licenses," as they were still called, were issued on prescribed conditions by clerks of court.[6] Finally, resort was had to formal centralization when, in 1853, the clerks were required to procure blank licenses from the Comptroller and to account for them with the utmost strictness.[7] The colonial plan of license control was thus revived with a more practical purpose, namely, the control of revenue.

In the colonial period and for some years after the Revolution the principal officers of some cities were appointed by

---

[1] E. L. Whitney, *J. H. U. Studies*, XIII, 104.

[2] *Laws of South Carolina* (in Library of Congress.)

[3] *Laws*, 1780, ch. 24.

[4] *Laws, Session of* 1827, ch. 117.

[5] *Laws*, 1853, ch. 86.

the central executive authority.   Mayors of cities, either independently or in conjunction with their boards of aldermen, were frequently empowered to grant liquor licenses.
In such cases a partial administrative control of license was
created which may be regarded as somewhat more practical
than in the case of administration by justices.   In the cities
of New York and Albany the mayor, recorder and aldermen had been constituted commissioners for collecting the
excise as early as 1753.[1]   When the excise system began to
be associated with the license system the same general plan
was followed, with modifications.   A complete license
system was first instituted for the commonwealth of New
York in 1788,[2] and it had a distinct flavor of city centralization.   The mayor of Albany and the mayor, recorder, aldermen and commonalty of Hudson were constituted excise
commissioners for their respective cities; while the single
excise commissioner provided for New York city four years
previously,[3] was now made an appointee of the governor.
That the commissioners were endowed with license powers
as well as powers of tax collection is evident from the discretion given them in connection with the detailed regula-
lations which the law imposed upon the traffic.   They were
required to consider the necessity of the place and the character of the person before granting a tavern license, and
might also fix the " duty of excise," within prescribed limits.[4]
There was thus worked out, especially in New York city, a
potentially definite administrative control of license, before
the beginning of the present century.

The policy of decentralization that followed with the
general triumph of radical democracy in the United States
was well illustrated in the license administration of New
York city.   At about the time when the mayor ceased to

[1] *Act of* Dec. 12, 1753.

[3] *Laws of* 1784, ch. 37.

[2] *Laws of* 1788, ch. 48.

[4] *Laws of* 1788, ch. 48.

be an appointee of the central administration, the license administration was given over to a peculiarly localized control. The city fathers having " by their petition, under their corporate seal, prayed for the passage of the following law," it was enacted that licenses should be granted and the fee of $10 collected in the several wards by the respective aldermen and assistants. No supervision of receipts and no accounting was required, and the proceeds were directed to be applied to the " support and maintenance of the poor of the city." [1]

II. *Current Forms*

In seeking to classify the various cases of central control of license we shall find it impracticable to follow the principle of relative efficiency. Efficiency being the object of centralization it might be expected that the more highly centralized forms would be the more efficient. Actual efficiency of administration is so largely determined by social and personal conditions that it cannot be assumed from the plan of administrative organization and the character of legal sanctions. Direct central administration of license was formal while it lasted and is now obsolete. The different forms of central control over the license functions of the local administration may be grouped best with reference to the degree to which license administration under central control has been specialized.

Liquor license administration is intimately related to penal police administration. The liquor traffic, directly or indirectly, affords more occasion for attention from peace officers than any other activity in which society is commonly concerned. In the United States the two branches of administration, commonly called " license " and " police," are so

[1] *Laws of* 1824, ch. 215. As amended (1825, ch. 196), the act practically excluded the interference of the mayor with the ward-administration of the respective aldermen.

generally regarded as belonging together that police boards
are frequently endowed with license functions. The result
is that other subjects of police activity are overshadowed,
and a branch of municipal administration has been developed
which might aptly be termed the department for the administration of liquor laws. Such consolidated systems naturally fall into a class distinct from simple license administration and may be considered separately.

The relation between license administration and revenue
administration, although naturally close, is of much less
significance than that between license and police. So long
as license powers are actually exercised in a discriminative
way for restrictive purposes, the collection of the fee, even
though it be so high as to amount to a considerable license
tax, is of secondary and even of slight importance as compared with the main object of the administration. When,
on the other hand, the excise is levied as a tax with only
incidental restriction, license functions cease to be significant
and are merged in revenue administration. In either case
the same officers may discharge both functions; but when
license officers also collect the incidental revenue their
revenue duties are so simple and ministerial as not to com-
plicate their functions. The administration of a liquor tax,
whether high or low, is analogous to that of a tariff on imports. The theoretic basis of a protective tariff is directly
opposed to that of a revenue tariff. Yet either may, in
practice, be made incidental to the other, and the same administrative organs may be employed for both purposes.
A strict license administration might rather be likened to an
immigration system in which a poll tax is imposed upon all
who enter, while some may be excluded through the exercise of a limited official discretion. License administration
may therefore be classified, without reference to revenue
functions, but with reference to its connection with police

functions, into: (1) Simple license administration, and (2) License combined with police administration.

Central control of license administration is found chiefly in cities. Virginia instituted in 1890 a system of centralized excise boards for all the cities of the commonwealth.[1] A central board, consisting of the auditor, second auditor and treasurer, was empowered " to elect for each city in the commonwealth three qualified voters " of the city, as a local board. The term of the local commissioners was to continue during the pleasure of the central board, which was empowered to fill all vacancies. Local commissioners were allowed a *per diem* compensation for actual service, to be paid from the commonwealth treasury. The powers of the boards respecting city liquor licenses were wide; they " may approve or disapprove the application as it seems right and proper to do;" an ultimate appeal from their decision might, however, be taken to the circuit court. The law was continued, with slight amendments, for several years, but has recently been repealed.

The preamble to the act creating this system sets forth that: " There exists in the cities of this commonwealth a growing dissatisfaction with the system under which licenses for the sale of ardent spirits are granted;" and that the legislature " is disposed to surround the granting of these licenses in large municipal corporations with all the safeguards suggested by an enlightened and progressive public policy." The auditor of public accounts, in answer to an inquiry as to the actual purpose and effect of the plan, says : " The Boards of Commissioners of Excise were created for a special purpose, which does not appear in the act defining their duties. This purpose they effectually accomplished

[1] *Act of* Feb. 25, 1890.

for several years and then, the conditions which had made their services useful having ceased to exist, they were abolished." [1]   The fact seems to be that revenue considerations were dominant in the instituting of the system.   Liquor license taxes form an important part of the central revenues of Virginia.   The general " license " act of 1890, applying to a wide variety of pursuits, provided, as previous tax laws had provided,[2] that the liquor excise should be paid in coin, United States treasury or national bank notes,[3] the object being to exclude coupons of Virginia bonds.   The central control was apparently established to insure the deposit of the authorized currency before issue of license, and thus to prevent the shrinkage of central revenue through connivance of local officers.

Central control of city license administration through a simple, single-headed commission is well illustrated in the system established by Missouri for the city of St. Louis. " There is hereby created," says the law, " the office of excise commissioner, who shall have exclusive authority to grant dramshop licenses; and the commissioner shall be appointed by and hold his office during the pleasure of the governor." [4]   The law empowers the commissioner to judge of the moral character of the applicant for license, as a ground of refusal to grant, and to revoke any license granted for violation of the dramshop laws.   " The excise commissioner," writes his deputy, " has discretionary powers; he can refuse a license where the applicant has filled all legal requirements if, in his opinion, the applicant is not a man of good moral character or . . . will not conduct an orderly house." [5]   A nominal control over the decision of the com-

[1] *Letter of* Sept. 20, 1898.   [2] See *Code of Va.* (1887) § 399.
[3] *Act of* March 6, 1890.   [4] *Act of* March 17, 1893.
[5] *Letter of* Sept. 17, 1898.

missioner is provided by a system of local option. On the
financial side the commissioner and the city collector serve
as mutual checks. The license tax is fixed, and accrues in
part to the commonwealth but chiefly to the city treasury,
the commissioner collecting, for compensation and expenses,
a separate fee of $3 for every semi-annual license issued by
him. The law contemplates the active coöperation of the
police with the commissioner. Notice of licenses issued is
to be given to the head of the police department. The partial centralization of police control, although distinct from
the centralized license administration, is doubtless conducive
to joint efficiency. Nevertheless, there is a serious disparity
between the number of licenses issued by the commissioner
and the number of special liquor taxes collected by the
United States internal revenue officers.[1] The commissioner
acknowledges the uniform support of the courts in prosecutions made ; but finds that " a large force of deputies and
detectives, under the immediate charge of the Commissioner," is necessary in making cases.[2]

Baltimore presents a well-developed system of simple
license administration by a centrally appointed board. The
board consists of three commissioners appointed by the
governor, with the approval of the senate, for a term of two
years.[3] As in the case of the license commissioner in St.
Louis, it is not even required that these commissioners shall
be residents of the city. No specific power of removal is
given the governor by the Maryland law. The salaries of
the commissioners, as well as " all salaries and expenses
necessarily incident to the business of the board," are paid
by the city of Baltimore. The authority of the board in
thus binding the city extends to the appointment of such

---

[1] F. H. Wines, in *The Liquor Problem*, p. 337.

[2] *Report*, Jan. 1, 1895.   [3] *Maryland Laws of* 1892, ch. 13.

clerks as it may need and to the fixing of their salaries. The license discretion of the board is practically unlimited. It may also revoke any license on the usual grounds " if sufficient cause shall at any time be shown or proof be made to the said board." [1]   For the purposes of all legal hearings and inquiries it may issue summons, administer oaths and require the coöperation of the city police in the service of summons. Here again the police administration is separately centralized.

The tone of a centralized branch of local administration naturally depends upon the tone of the administrative head. A prominent citizen of Baltimore writes, in answer to inquiry: " The liquor license commissioners under the old régime here were always unscrupulous and usually disreputable politicians: since 1895 they have been politicians, but of much better antecedents and reputation. . . . It is usually easy now to get licenses refused when there is strong opposition in the neighborhood.". [2]

2. LICENSE COMBINED WITH POLICE ADMINISTRATION

An excise board for the metropolitan police district was constituted by the legislature of New York in 1866. [3] It consisted of the five commissioners of the metropolitan sanitary district and the four commissioners of metropolitan police. The sanitary commission was made up of three residents of New York city and one resident of Brooklyn, appointed by the Governor, together with the health officer of the port of New York. [4] The police commissioners, originally appointed by the Governor, [5] were at this time elected by the legislature. [6] The excise board thus consti-

---

[1] *Laws of* 1890, ch. 343.

[2] *Letter of* C. J. Bonaparte, Sept. 19, 1898.

[3] *Laws of* 1866, ch. 578.   [4] *Laws of* 1866, ch: 74.

[5] *Laws of* 1857, ch. 569.   [6] *Laws of* 1864, ch. 41.

tuted was identical with the metropolitan board of health which had been established a few weeks earlier;[1] while its territorial jurisdiction included the entire metropolitan police district[2] with the exception of the county of Westchester.

The excise board was given the powers exercised under the general license law of 1857 by the several county boards, including discretion as to persons, places and fees, the limits of fees in the city being $30 and $250.[3] In addition, the metropolitan excise board was given authority, not granted in the general law, to license places for the sale of liquors "to be drunk on the premises, the same not being inns, taverns or hotels." It could also appoint an inspector, at a salary of $2000, and employ attorneys to prosecute violations. All fees and penalties collected were to be credited to the metropolitan police department.

One of the authors of the metropolitan excise law states, in answer to inquiry, that it was enacted not on account of local official corruption, but simply on account of the indifference of local authorities to the enforcement of law. Official zeal in local administration could hardly have been expected in excise matters when the privilege of self-government had been withdrawn in nearly all other important branches of city administration. The centralized excise system was a logical concomitant of the other parts of the "metropolitan" scheme, and it disappeared with them in 1870.[4]

The most elaborate development of central control of joint police and license administration is found in Boston, and one or two other cities of Massachusetts. The organization and police powers of the Boston board of police are concisely set forth in the words of the constituent act:[5]

---

[1] *Laws of* 1866, ch. 74.   [2] See Chapter III.   [3] *Laws of* 1857, ch. 628.
[4] *Laws of* 1870, ch. 175.   [5] *Acts of* 1885, ch. 323.

The governor of the commonwealth with the advice and consent of
the council shall appoint from the two principal political parties
three citizens of Boston . . . who shall constitute a board of police
for said city. . . . One member of said board shall be designated
by the governor as chairman. . . . The full term of office shall be
five years. . . . The members of said board may be removed by
the governor with the advice and consent of the council for such
cause as he shall deem sufficient and shall express in the order of
removal. . . . The board of police shall have authority to appoint
and establish and organize the police of said city of Boston and
make all needful rules and regulations for its efficiency. . . . All
expenses shall be paid by the city of Boston upon the requisition of
said board. The board of police shall make a detailed report of its
doings quarterly to the mayor of said city and annually to the governor of the commonwealth. . . . In case of tumult, riot or violent
disturbance of public order the mayor of said city shall have, as the
exigency in his judgment may require, the right to assume control,
for the time being, of the police of the said city.

The license powers of the board are defined, in the main,
by general laws and include full discretion as respects persons and places as well as the power of revocation for cause.[1]
Administrative discretion as to number of licenses is qualified, nominally by local option, and positively by statutory
limitation of the number of licenses according to population.

The " metropolitan " system in Boston was established in
obedience to a strong popular demand for efficient enforcement of liquor laws. The license régime inaugurated in
Massachusetts in 1875 after prohibition had reigned, if not
ruled, for a generation, was difficult of enforcement. This
was especially the case in cities, where illicit traffic had
flourished in the face of prohibitory laws. License administration in cities was committed to the mayor and aldermen,
with the option given them of appointing special license

---

[1] *Acts of* 1875, ch. 99; *Public Statutes*, ch. 100.

commissioners.[1]   In Boston, license commissioners were appointed and served as a separate board until 1878.   Legislative control was freely exercised.   The edition of "Statutes and Ordinances" of Boston for 1876 contains this suggestive note as to license regulations: "These acts are not included in this digest, as they are liable to be changed from year to year both in form and substance."   In 1878 the police administration of Boston, which had previously been under the immediate control of the mayor and aldermen, was committed to a new local board of police commissioners.[2]   The same act transferred to this board the powers of the license commissioners.   The resulting administration of liquor laws was extremely lax.   "For three consecutive years the common council of Boston had a 'committee on police' which had to deal with the confirmation of gentlemen appointed as members of the police commission, with all appropriations for police purposes and with all matters of city legislation relating to police, and during the whole three years that committee was composed of two retail liquor dealers and another member in full sympathy with the interest."[3]   A Citizens' Law and Order League was organized in 1882, "to secure a better enforcement of the restrictive features of existing laws for the regulation of the liquor traffic."   The re-establishment and extension of the general commonwealth control of local police was strongly urged.   The Boston police bill was accepted as a compromise.   The system thus instituted has stood practically unchanged, and seems at present to be more strongly established than ever.

[1] *Acts of* 1875, ch. 99.

[2] *Act of* May 14, 1878, ch. 244.

[3] *Bulletin of Law and Order League,* June, 1892. See also *The Liquor Problem,* p. 191, and testimony of H. H. Faxon and others before the Legislative Committee on the liquor law, Feb. 23, 1882.

The permanency of this plan in Boston makes it a peculiarly valuable object of study with respect to the relations of centralized license and police administration. In the matter of license administration proper, the question of local sentiment is of primary importance. A central control having been established to obviate the evil effects of local influences, the question is presented whether or not the better element of the community will find its wishes also flouted by an irresponsible bureaucracy? On the general question of license or no-license the city votes as a whole; and there has seldom been room for doubt as to the result in Boston.[1] The unofficial analysis of the vote, showing opposition to the saloon in certain sections, backed by personal remonstrance against the grant of license on the part of residents, has had influence with the board in the distribution of licenses. The Dorchester district had 30 saloons in 1885; in 1895 the number had been reduced to 3. Other influences, however, enter. The statutory limitation of the number of licenses to 1 for every 500 of population[2] has not only reduced the number of saloons, but has by practical implication fixed a minimum as well as a maximum. Active local sentiment may expel saloons from the Back Bay residence district, but a passive local sentiment is compelled to receive a corresponding excess in the North End.[3] In consequence of the rigid limitation, renewals are the rule and the right of transfer becomes a valuable one.

The union of license and police functions in a centralized board has given rise to much controversy apart from the general question of centralized administration. One of the commissioners on the Boston board of police, speaking for the board, has expressed his conviction that a union of some

---

[1] The vote in 1897, a fairly typical one, was: Yes, 43,719; No, 26,177.

[2] *Acts of* 1888, ch. 340.

[3] *Cf.* "*Substitutes for the Saloon*," Prof. F. G. Peabody, *Forum*, July, 1896.

sort is essential to efficient license administration. General experience confirms this opinion. Massachusetts herself has recently illustrated this view, without reference to centralization, by transferring the police administration of the city of Lowell to the license commission, and providing that the commission should be known as "the board of police."[1] The policy is not peculiar; the manner, only, is striking. The result, also, seems fairly typical, in kind if not in degree, if we may credit the testimony of the board in its report two years later, as follows:[2]

The conduct of the liquor traffic has in the past been a source of anxiety and trouble to the police department; but during the incumbency of the Police Board the laws governing the traffic have been strictly and impartially enforced, and not a single violation of the law by a licensed dealer has occurred.

The estimated population of Lowell in 1897 was 90,000. The records of the police board in Boston show in a graphic way the extent to which the liquor traffic is involved in the work of the police. The following figures are taken from the annual reports of the board to the governor:

	1894	1895	1896	1897
Total Arrests....................	42,035	42,534	48,796	45,659
Assault......................	2,888	2,702	3,098	2,976
Drunkenness..	25,063	26,185	31,200	29,643
Violation of Liquor Law...........	648	683	500	242
Total	28,599	29,570	34,798	32,861

Thus, on an average, about 70 per cent. of the arrests made are closely connected with the sale and use of intoxicating liquors. In this table several minor classes of cases are

[1] *Acts of* 1895, ch. 187.

[2] *Report of the Lowell Board of Police*, 1897.

omitted, which might be included as more or less closely related to the liquor traffic. It is believed that this omission substantially offsets the error of excess arising from the inclusion of all cases of assault.

The results of centralized administration in Boston in both its restrictive and its repressive branches may be estimated from the data contained in the reports of the board of police, from other official declarations, from the testimony of private persons and from personal observation. The reports of the board indicate a great improvement in the respect for law shown by licensed dealers. In 1886, the first year of the centralized control, 267 complaints were filed against licensees, of which 108 resulted in the forfeiture of the license. In 1896 there were but 12 complaints, with 3 forfeitures. The figures of complaints in other recent years, viz., 26 in 1894, 20 in 1895, and 15 in 1897, indicate a steady decrease which is quite out of proportion to the reduction in number of licenses resulting from the limitation law. The reports show a corresponding improvement in judicial procedure—an improvement which had been sought without practical result through repeated legislative mandates, as, for instance, the requirement that cases must proceed to trial and judgment.[1] Effective special measures have been adopted for the repression of illicit traffic. Here the board found its police powers peculiarly serviceable. In 1895 a " liquor squad," comprising one captain of police, one sergeant and fifteen men, " selected with especial reference to the efficient performance of this duty," was set apart by the board for service specifically in the enforcement of liquor laws. The report for 1896 says: " There are few if any kitchen bar-rooms in Boston, no open houses of ill repute and not a gambling house doing business anywhere

---

[1] *Act of* 1885, ch. 359, and prior acts referred to. Cf. *The Liquor Problem*, p. 210.

in the city—which is largely due to the energy and excellent work of this squad."

While allowance must be made for unconscious color in this interested testimony, the general proposition that the liquor laws are well enforced is supported by testimony from critical sources. In 1892 the Citizens' Law and Order League of Massachusetts put forth this statement concerning Boston: " Liquor licenses are no longer granted or refused according as the applicant has or lacks political influence. Members of the force no longer rely upon ' political pull ' for promotion, but understand that faithful service in the execution of all the laws is the only road to a more desirable place. . . . It is by far the best police system to be found in any large city in this country." [1] Perhaps the best attestation to this testimony is the fact that this league, which for ten years had been active in promoting legislation and administration to restrain the liquor traffic, has now practically gone out of existence. Temperance organizations are still active in Boston ; but the administration of the laws has ceased to be their most pressing concern. Their leaders admit, in 1898, that, although there is room for improvement, the liquor laws in general are better enforced than ever before.

The city government of Boston is usually in the hands of the party opposed to that which controls the commonwealth government, and opposed, also, by its general principles, to centralization. When William E. Russell, the only representative of that party who has occupied the office of governor since 1883, was elected governor in 1890, he manifested hostility to the plan of control of Boston police. Unquestionably there were grounds for criticism at that time which have since been removed, although Governor Russell himself could secure but little improvement, owing

[1] *Bulletin of the Tenth Annual Meeting.*

to the political opposition of both council and legislature. The general tone of the commonwealth government of Massachusetts is high, despite the fact that one party is reasonably sure of continued control. To Governor Frederick T. Greenhalge is due great credit for the efficiency of the Boston police board. In 1894, acting against partisan pressure and, as was generally recognized, for the betterment of the local administration, he appointed as chairman of the board a gentleman of the opposition party, supplanting a member of his own party. In his address to the legislature of 1896, Governor Greenhalge said:

The board of police in Boston gives a large measure of security and order to the city. If the always vexatious question of liquor licenses could be placed upon some impersonal and non-partisan basis a great advance might be made, consistent with and supported by public opinion. If every applicant could be graded or rated in such a way as to give weight to character, to previous history or record, to location and similar features, the struggle for licenses might be relieved from some of its more objectionable features. In fact, though a suggestion of civil service rules in such cases might seem ironical, some system which would eliminate political and pernicious influences is to be desired.

Friction between the city government and the police board has been pronounced, at times. Mayor Mathews complained, in his elaborate valedictory address, that the withdrawal of police control from the city authorities interfered with the proper enforcement of ordinances. "The transfer," he continues, " of a purely local concern, such as the police force of a city, to the control of the commonwealth is a violation of the principle of local self-government and a constant source of irritation to the people. The gain in efficiency, if any, is not commensurate with the breach of principle." [1] Since the administration of Mayor Mathews

[1] *The City Government of Boston*, by Nathan Mathews.

there has been less friction. His implied admission of an increased efficiency, owing to central control, is generally endorsed as a fact. His present successor, Mayor Quincy, has courteously given an informal expression of his views on the subject, substantially as follows : [1]

I am free to say that, under the present board, police administration has been better, the laws have been more strictly enforced, good order has been more generally maintained than under the old system. When the tone of the state government is higher than that of the city government, centralized police administration is the better system. The strictly police functions are more properly a state affair than most of the other departments of city government. The artificial limit placed by law upon the number of licenses to be granted gives rise to a pressure upon the board, as a liquor license board, that tends to demoralize the whole system. The police board would be less exposed to corrupting influences if license functions were set off from it—but to confer license powers on a board locally chosen would produce less satisfactory results than the present plan. The qualifications should be prescribed by law and the fee fixed high enough to limit the number naturally.

The license laws of Massachusetts being stringent in a high degree, their enforcement would presumably be difficult, especially in the metropolis. A tour of the saloons of the First Police Division, comprising the Italian quarter and the most active section of the water-front, during holiday week, leads one to the conclusion that the law is enforced in Boston with great punctiliousness, while relations of mutual respect subsist between the police and the people. The night- and Sunday-closing laws seem to be well observed. In the matter of illicit traffic the manifest thoroughness of police surveillance indicates that the reports of the police board correctly reflect the actual situation. In general, comparative statistics of arrests for different periods are not

[1] *Interview*, Feb. 11, 1898.

to be trusted. Fewer arrests may mean only that the town is run on the "wide open" policy. The decrease in arrests for "violation of liquor law" as shown in the table on page 51, seems, however, only a fair indication of increased police efficiency, especially since the organization of the "liquor squad."

The attempts of the friends of "law and order," to extend the Boston plan to smaller cities has elicited a discussion of the merits of the system as a general scheme aside from its application to a metropolitan district. The most notable of these attempts was that which resulted in establishing the Fall River board of police in 1894.[1] The division in the legislature on the passage of the Fall River bill was closely on party lines, about two-thirds of each house sustaining it. Three of the five representatives from Fall River were ranged with the minority against the bill. The minority urged that the motive behind the proposition was not good government, but partisan advantage through centralization; that the proposition was un-American and un-democratic in making the city the ward of the commonwealth: "If she burns her fingers," they said, "let her learn to keep them out of the fire." The majority replied that the plea for local self-government was out of place when the city, through its constituted authorities, set aside sovereign laws of the commonwealth; that the "best element" of the city were at the mercy of the "rum element," and that the right to be clean and pure was a divine right, to be guaranteed by the commonwealth. An opponent of the bill, admitting that the liquor interest had demoralized the city government, contended that the liquor traffic and not the entire police of the city should be subjected to centralized administrative control. A Boston senator, on the other hand, avowed that, having been brought up in the

[1] *Acts of* 1894, ch. 351.

liquor business and followed it in the city for many years, he
" never felt safer or more secure" than under the police commission appointed by the governor; instead therefore of
attempting merely to eliminate the liquor license administration from local politics, he would vote broadly to emancipate
local politics from the liquor traffic.[1] Amendments proposed
with a view to making the effect of the act conditional upon
its acceptance by the voters of the city were rejected.[2]   A
separate proposition to establish boards of license commissioners, to be appointed by the governor, in cities generally
was also seriously discussed in the legislature.[3]

The expediency and the limits of central intervention, in
city license and police administration, were lucidly discussed
by Governor Greenhalge in his veto message on a measure,
passed by his own party in the legislature, to establish a
miniature Boston board of police in the city of Holyoke.
The following is an excerpt :[4]

It is clear that the governor must always come to this task under
disadvantages.   He can seldom have personal knowledge of the
candidates; he must depend upon others, who are often partisans
or interested parties, for information ; his judgment must often be at
second hand.   But the important principle of local self-government—the autonomy of city or town—is a material factor in this
inquiry.   Every citizen may claim the right of trial by a jury of the
vicinage, and, while the guardians of the public peace are agents of
the commonwealth, it has always been deemed best, except in special
extraordinary cases, that they should be selected by the local authorities who have the best means of knowing their qualifications, and
that those who have the best means of observing the manner in which
officials discharge their duty should have the power of appointment

---

[1] *Boston Herald: Daily reports of legislative proceedings*, March and April,
1894.

[2] *Journals : Senate and House*, April, 1894.

[3] *Boston Transcript*, May 2, 1894.

[4] *Special Messages*, 1895.

and removal.   The case of the city of Holyoke does not seem to be analogous to that of the city of Boston or of the city of Fall River. The former is not only the city of Boston, but may be regarded as in a certain degree the city of Massachusetts, in which many persons not legal citizens thereof have vast property or business interests, and which every citizen of Massachusetts visits more or less frequently and in which all take peculiar and profound interest.   In the city of Fall River the friends of law and order appeared for a time to be unable to make head against selfish and demoralizing influences, and were compelled to ask the aid of the commonwealth to assist them in the great and unusual emergency.   The city of Holyoke appears to have within itself the vital and recuperative energy requisite to effect its own complete deliverance.

The validity of the Boston police law was tested in a case which arose involving the authority of the board to grant licenses for certain occupations previously licensed by the local authorities.   The Supreme Judicial Court, in its opinion, discussed the question of rights of local government in part as follows:[1]

The several towns and cities are agencies of government largely under the control of the legislature.   The powers and duties of all the towns and cities except so far as they are specifically provided for in the constitution are created and defined by the legislature, and we have no doubt that it has the right in its discretion to change the powers and duties created by itself and to vest such powers and duties in officers appointed by the governor if in its judgment the public good requires this, instead of leaving officers to be elected by the people or appointed by the municipal authorities.

License powers are in some cases committed to police boards consisting only in part of commissioners appointed by the central executive.   In Kansas City, Missouri, the board consists of the mayor for the time being and two other persons appointed by the governor for three-year

[1] Commonwealth *v*. Plaisted, 148 *Mass.*, 375.

terms and removable by him. By a separate provision of
the Kansas City charter, this police board is authorized to
grant dramshop licenses. The license powers of this board
are substantially the same as those of the excise commissioner in St. Louis. Both discharge functions committed,
by the general liquor license law of the commonwealth, to
the county court.[1]

This plan of police organization has existed in Kansas
City since 1875. The freeholders' charter of 1889 embodied the provision for central appointment. In 1898 an
amendment to the charter was proposed by the common
council, repealing this provision, substituting commissioners
elected by the voters of the city, and also creating a separate
excise board. Injunction proceedings were begun to stop
the vote on the ground of the unconstitutionality of the proposed repeal by the city of a commonwealth law. The
proceedings were dropped, however, and the proposed
amendment was defeated at the polls.[2] The people pre-
ferred the continuance of central control. This is not to be
interpreted as popular support of strict administration.
Neither is it a matter of partisan predilection, for the city
usually elects a mayor of a party opposed to that which
controls the commonwealth government. It is generally
understood that a lax administration of liquor laws prevails
in Kansas City, and the voters prefer that it continue so.
Comparative freedom of the liquor traffic offers double
advantage to the commercial interests involved in it.
Kansas City, Kansas, the largest city of that prohibition
commonwealth, is just across the border. Part of the
boundary line betweeen the two commonwealths runs
through the heart of one great commercial organism. The

---

[1] *Mo. R. S.* (1889), § 4572.

[2] *Letter of* H. C. Ward, Police Commissioner, Sept. 21, 1898.

ban placed upon the traffic west of the line puts a premium on commercial activity where it is permitted and tends to make the liquor interest aggressive and dominant. At the same time, the inevitable springing up of "joints" for illicit traffic, which is always found in urban territory under prohibitory laws, incites an unholy rivalry on the part of unlicensed traffic east of the line. A well informed correspondent residing in Kansas City, Kansas, writes: "If such a thing is possible, the license law on that side of the line is more loosely enforced than is the prohibitory one on this side."[1] Low local standards of liquor law enforcement seem to prevail in this case against the theoretic efficiency of a centralized administration; and the support given the centralized administration by the local electorate indicates that the reason of this failure is the fact that central standards and local standards are practically in accord.

Centralized systems are subject to the vicissitudes of party politics, especially in the west, where waves of radicalism extend to the whole field of legislation. In Nebraska a board of fire and police commissioners was created for Omaha in 1887,[2] consisting of three electors of the city, to be appointed by a central board consisting of the governor, the commissioner of public lands and buildings and the attorney-general, and to be subject to removal by the same authority. To this board of fire and police commissioners was also committed the license administration. The motive of the enactment seems to have been, at least in part, a desire for efficient administration; and this object was, in a considerable measure, realized. In 1897, a new party having come into control of the commonwealth government, the board of fire and police commissioners was reorganized with a membership consisting of the mayor and four appointees

[1] *Letter of* Feb. 12, 1898.   [2] *Laws of* 1887, ch. 10.

of the governor.[1]   At the same session a new board of fire
and police commissioners, which was also endowed with
license powers, was created for the city of Lincoln, to consist
of three persons appointed by the governor.[2]   Elaborate
provision was made for complaints and discipline, as follows:

For official misconduct the governor may remove any of said commissioners; any person aggrieved by any act of said commissioners
may file written charges against such commissioner or commissioners
with the governor, who shall within a reasonable time investigate the
same upon testimony produced before him and shall make a finding
as to the truth or falsity of such charges. . . .

Within a few months a hostile Supreme Court, on an action
of *quo warranto*, decided, on technical grounds, that the
grant of license powers to the Lincoln board was invalid.[3]
Recently, on an action of *quo warranto* instituted by a pre-
sumptive board of fire and police commissioners appointed
by the mayor of Omaha, the act of 1897 applying to that
city was declared unconstitutional, as being an attempt to
deprive the people of local self-government.[4]

III. *Theory*

The theory of centralized police administration, in its repressive and penal features, will be touched upon in the next
chapter.   We may here note some principles underlying
the forms of centralized control which have been considered:
(1) in the field of restrictive license administration; (2)
with reference to the union of license and police administration under central control.

It should first be noted that the perplexing problem pre-

[1] *Laws of* 1897, ch. 10.

[2] *Laws of* 1897, ch. 14.

[3] State *v.* Tibbetts, 52 *Nebr.*, 228.

[4] State *v.* Moores, 76 *N. W. Rep.*, 175.   See this decision for citations of other
instances of police centralization and an exhaustive discussion of the principle.

sented in the historical development of current forms of license administration is still in process of solution. We still have before us examples of judicial administration of license as well as of the other two kinds which comprise most cases, viz.: the police-license administration and the specialized license admininstration. In some commonwealths, especially in the south, license functions remain with the petty courts, as a sort of administrative annex to their judicial functions. This is a mere historic survival. In a very few, as in Pennsylvania, courts of quarter sessions exercise license functions,[1] apparently because of the compatibility between the deliberative temper of a court of justice and the discriminative character of the license function. By a suggestive coincidence it has also become the custom in some parts of Pennsylvania for the managers of a political party to call upon occupants of the bench to name the candidate of the party for a non-judicial office, a practice which has, in particular cases, elicited trenchant criticism, such as the following, from an independent press: " Mud will be thrown at them, and mud will stick even to ermine. This has been sadly evident in the operation of the Brooks liquor license law. One of the chosen judges is sufficient of a politician already, without being encouraged."[2] The effort to keep the liquor interest out of politics by committing the license function to the judiciary may, for a time, be well for the license administration, but it bodes ill for the continued high character of the bench.[3] This plan seeks to carry license administration in a right course by the sheer momentum of the judicial responsibilities to which it is annexed. It admits of no development of administrative control.

[1] *Act of* May 13, 1887 (ch. 108).

[2] *Pittsburg Dispatch*, Sept. 19, 1898.

[3] *C f. 'The Liquor Problem*,' p. 240.

Separate license administration is seldom centralized. When centralized it is usually associated with revenue administration in some controlling relation. Separate excise or license commissions are frequently found as a branch of local administration, especially in cities, but their short-comings are more likely to become apparent through loss of revenue or disturbance of the peace than through any direct channels of public perception from the license administration proper. Hence centralized control, when there is occasion to institute it, usually proceeds on lines of revenue or police administration, with license conjoined. Moreover, the judicial tradition persists, though license be ranked among the administrative departments. While the king stood as the fountain of justice, all judicial functions might be subject to his control. It has been difficult to establish the control of the commonwealth executive over even a *quasi*-judicial department of local government. The *quasi*-judicial activities of the central commonwealth government stand on a different basis. There has been a marked tendency to commit to special administrative boards *quasi*-judicial functions requiring technical knowledge, as, for example, the supervision and adjudication of railroad tariffs, and, in a less discriminative but more deliberative sphere, the equalization of taxes. The functions of such central boards are largely general and impersonal; the functions of a license board, on the other hand, are essentially special in application and personal in their exercise. If the license board exercises discretion, the only practical basis of judgment must be personal knowledge of local facts. A license board must discharge the duties of both jury and court for the purpose of adjudication between an individual who applies for a license and the local community which will be affected by it. Every canon of normal self-government re-quires that in such a case the discriminative judgment with which, under a general law, choice is made among individuals in granting privileges of trade, should reflect the consensus of the community. Every extraneous administrative element introduced to control the choice tends to derange the system. If abnormal local conditions have already deranged the system, artificial readjustment through outside control may be necessary.

If license administration were separately centralized in a large city, without the support of the police force, it could permit, but could not prevent. Presumably the conditions which warranted central control of license would also affect the efficiency of the police. Indeed, such an arrangement would be so nugatory as a means of improved administration, unless as a mere check on revenue, that there appears to be no notable instance of its being attempted without a corresponding central control of police administration. It only remains, therefore, to consider, in this chapter, the theory of city police centralization in so far as it affects a centralized license administration. This topic presents itself in two forms: (1) license and police administration coördinately centralized; and (2) license and police administration consolidated under central control. Some preliminary considerations, however, apply to both.

The necessity of central administrative intervention in the control of the liquor traffic is usually deduced from the importance of breaking a circuit of vicious influences, whereby the saloon, as an institution, controls voters, voters elect the local authorities, and the local authorities appoint and direct the officers of the law. By putting the officer under central responsibility and local irresponsibility, he is freed, to a great extent, from the force of politico-personal influence that can be brought to bear by directly interested parties. The principle cuts both ways: the officer is no more bound to observe the better sentiment of the community than he is free to disregard the wishes of the vicious element. Influences may also operate on the central administrative head similar to those which corrupt local authorities. The whole scheme may seem to be a mere removal of the place of barter from the city hall to the state-house. This very removal, however, puts the field of action upon a higher plane. Unquestionably the centralization of excise administration to any considerable extent means ultimately little more than the forming of a new line of battle. But in this respect the development is consistent with the trend of the time toward concentration; and posterity must take care of its own problems. At the same time it must be remembered that central responsibility enlists in the interest of good administration the moral sense of the whole commonwealth. Even the largest of our cities contains only half the population of the commonwealth, and commands dignity, opportunity and accountability in about the same ratio. Whatever the inducements that may be offered the governor to favor particular interests in the metropolis, they cannot be brought to bear upon him with such direct force as upon the mayor whose entire constituency is in the field of their immediate influence. The governor is, at least in part, outside the vicious circle.

These considerations are obviously of no significance as applied to a commonwealth executive who is disposed to favor lax administration and believes that his constituency at large will uphold him in such a course. Such a state of things is not only possible but seems in some cases to be actual; but it is abnormal if not unusual. In the first place, the city, in consequence of modern conditions of industry and trade, gathers out of the commonwealth the elements that most need government, and throws them into social conditions such that they are least able to govern themselves. Presumably the political morals of the commonwealth at large are left better than those of the city; and in that case it is only a due return that the commonwealth should help the city bear the unequal burden of government which has been thrown upon it. In the second place, when a commonwealth supports its chief executive in his connivance at the violation of law, the law is no longer law. It is a dead letter, and will be formally repealed unless retained for ulterior reasons or with the tacit understanding that, in some communities, it is not to be enforced because it cannot be enforced either by central or by local officers.

(1.) Coördinate centralization of license and police administration offers some advantages. Coördinate bodies concerned in the different phases of liquor law enforcement are not only a check upon each other, but are less easily controlled by corrupt influence than a single body. The differing terms of office in separate boards, whereby the appointees are likely to hold from different occupants of the central executive chair, make it less likely that the central executive control will be used to further personal ends. The specialization of function thus secured also makes central administrative control more easy to establish, as well as more likely to be maintained.

(2.) Joint centralization of police and license administration concentrates responsibility for the enforcement of liquor laws. It subordinates all other objects of police activity to this one object, and, as statistics of arrests show, with some good reason. But the tables of arrests tell hardly half the story. License implies restraint, restraint implies desire, and desire calls for watchfulness corresponding to the strength and wide-spread dominance of the desire. In a large city the liquor traffic tends to spring up everywhere, and where it is licensed it tends to break over the limitations which license has imposed. It is the regularity of the policeman on his beat, with an independent police board behind him, rather than detective work and special raids, that has reduced the violations of the conditions of license to insignificant proportions in Boston. The "liquor squad" has its place; but the liquor law is enforced by the police force as a whole. It could not be enforced without them; its enforcement is, in fact, though largely negative, the major part of their duties, and its efficient enforcement is secured in large measure through concentration of responsibility.

CHAPTER III

REPRESSIVE POLICE ADMINISTRATION

THE activity of the administration in keeping the peace and in securing the punishment of those who violate the law occupies a large place in the legal relations of the liquor traffic. The liquor traffic, in turn, would fill a large place in a general discussion of this branch of administrative activity. Were we concerned with mere local administration of liquor laws, this field would be extremely broad. By the introduction of the element of centralization the subject is simplified as well as narrowed; for centralized control of police administration has in most instances been instituted, either exclusively or very largely, for the more efficient enforcement of liquor laws.

The field of legislation upon this subject may be likened to an ellipse, its two foci being the principle of prohibition and the problem of city government; both of which have become important, as legislative points of view, within the last half-century. The subject has, therefore, properly speaking, no history. All its characteristic forms are essentially current. Such an institution as a centralized constabulary was unknown in the colonies and during the first half-century of democracy in America.[1] Even in England, systematic central supervision of the local peace through subsidies and inspection was not established until after the middle of this century.[2] In England the control of the

[1] *Cf.* Howard, *Local Constitutional History of the United States, passim.*

[2] *Cf.* Maltbie, *English Local Government of To-day,* p. 121.

68   [406

rural constabulary by the county magistracy, who, in turn, were nominated by the Lord Lieutenant, secured no effective administrative control, while it sacrificed local accountability.[1] In the United States the constables were under purely local responsibility, as a rule, both in towns and in cities.

The American idea of a constabulary is a police force under central control, organized for service throughout the commonwealth. Centralized administration of the police force of a particular city, on the other hand, is commonly called a system of metropolitan police, because originally applied, in the United States, to the principal city of a commonwealth, or because of the connection of the term with the metropolitan police district about London. The constabulary is general, the metropolitan system is local. For this reason the constabulary is usually found in connection with a general, repressive plan of regulation, such as prohibition or the commonwealth dispensary system. Either form of administration may be definitely set up by legislation or conditionally provided, to be put in operation in the discretion of the central executive. Both forms are positive, in that an actual exercise of appointing power is involved. Over against them must be placed the comparatively negative control exercised through central supervision and direction of local officers, a power which is sometimes sanctioned with the authority of suspension or removal. Those commonwealths in which repressive liquor legislation has assumed the most radical forms and has withstood the most violent opposition—especially Maine, Kansas and South Carolina—have each had recourse to a variety of forms of centralized police control.

[1] *Cf.* Mullins, Edw.: *The Magistracy of England.* London, 1836.

I. *Development and Current Forms*

I. CENTRAL SUPERVISION AND DIRECTION

For reasons peculiar to American polity this sort of control generally amounts to nothing. In the United States the system of control through subsidies has not been developed in the field of police administration. The authority given to the governor in some commonwealths to suspend mayors, sheriffs and prosecuting attorneys for malfeasance or nonfeasance, it would seem, might be made a powerful means of control in the hands of an able and conscientious executive. The merely temporary operation of such authority, however, together with the unpleasantness of the task, especially in the absence of the positive power of appointment, usually deters the governor from exercising his authority. If this sort of control does not develop into a more positive form, it usually degenerates into legislative control, which means either a derangement of local government by acts of special application, or great detail in prescribing general rules of administrative action.

The difficulties of central supervision and direction without the sanctions of administrative control are illustrated in the history of the so-called sheriff law of Maine,[1] enacted especially to secure the enforcement of prohibition. The first section provides that " It shall be the duty of sheriffs to obey all such orders and directions relating to the enforcement and execution of the laws of the state as they shall from time to time receive from the governor." The specific duties of sheriffs and county attorneys respecting the enforcement of the liquor laws are detailed; then, in the final section, instead of summary powers of discipline, one finds the following: " Whenever the governor shall, after investigation, be satisfied that any sheriff or county attorney has wilfully refused or neglected to discharge the duties imposed

---

[1] *Act of* Feb. 29, 1872.

upon each by this act, it shall be his duty to bring such fact to the attention of the legislature at the earliest practicable day." [1]

A fair estimate of the efficacy of central supervision and direction in Maine may be obtained by putting together an unofficial, typical news-item and the comment of the governor thereon. The item is headed, " Practically a license system in Maine," and reads, in part, as follows:

The long-heralded hearing before Governor Powers on the question of the non-enforcement of the Maine prohibitory law took place in the Houlton court house.   Mr. H———, in presenting the petitions, stated that there is a growing impression that the dominant party in the state of Maine does not want the prohibition law enforced, that the judges of the supreme court do not want it enforced, and that, as the officers charged with its enforcement take their cue from the leaders, the result is a flagrant violation of the law throughout the state, with a shameful non-enforcement of the penalties provided by law.

Upon request for a statement concerning the incident, the governor courteously responded, in part as follows: [2]

It is the duty of the governor of the state to direct all officers to enforce the laws. I issued letters to the several sheriffs in response to the meeting with the Civic League. I have full power, on petition of thirty tax-payers, to appoint what are known as state constables, to enforce the prohibitory law, as many as are desired. I stated to the petitioners that while it was a part of my duty to request and command all sheriffs to enforce the laws, that in case they refused to do so, I had no power of removal; that they were not appointed by me but elected by the people, and responsible to the people in their several counties for their acts. This has been the condition of things in Maine since 1855. In case they do not fulfil their duties they are subject to impeachment, but they cannot be removed by me unless they have been impeached. The prohibitory law is not

[1] A strong amendment respecting control over county attorneys has since been enacted. See Chapter V.

[2] *Letter of* Feb. 3, 1899.

enforced as it should be in our larger cities and towns, but it is very thoroughly enforced in our country towns.[1]

Similar conditions, under a different form of organization, formerly existed in Rhode Island. When prohibition, in 1886, after having been repealed twice, was given a new brief lease of life, the supervision of its enforcement was committed to a "chief of state police," elected by the general assembly, in grand committee, and commissioned by the governor.[2] All sheriffs, town-sergeants, constables and municipal police officers, constituting the "state police," were, in the general enforcement of the prohibitory law, subject to the direction of the chief. The legislative provision making all local officers of the law a "state police" was not confined to the prohibition era, and is an interesting recognition of the abstract doctrine that all such officers are agents of the commonwealth. It is still made "their special duty to use their utmost efforts to repress and prevent crime by the suppression of all unlicensed liquor shops," etc.[3] The legislature, in grand committee, still elects the sheriff for each county,[4] and the sheriff is specially directed to ap-

---

[1] In Great Britain, under the system of grants, central supervision has been made more generally effective than in the United States. A letter of instructions or of censure from the central executive means much more when the hand that writes it also holds the purse-strings. For instance, in Wigan, a small place, the chief constable and other constables being notoriously hand in glove with the liquor interest, the following admonition, in a letter of Jan. 25, 1897, from the Home Office to the town clerk, was deemed sufficient: "It appears to him [the Secretary] that the condition of the force is by no means wholly satisfactory, and will require careful watching by the responsible authorities. . . . I am to add that Sir Matthew Ridley entertains no doubt that the members of the Watch Committee are fully alive to the necessity of careful and efficient supervision for the purpose of establishing a satisfactory state of discipline in the force under their control."—*Minutes of Evidence, Royal Commission on the Liquor Licensing Laws*, Vol. II., § 20,850.

[2] *Acts of* 1886, ch. 596.   [3] *Gen. Laws of R. I.* (1896), ch. 102, § 17.

[4] *Gen. Laws of R. I.* (1896), ch. 24, § 6.

point a deputy to see to the enforcement of the liquor laws.[1]

The dispensary law of South Carolina, in addition to its more direct means of centralized enforcement, undertakes to secure the coöperation of local officers by providing that " Any constable, deputy constable, sheriff or magistrate who shall neglect or refuse to perform the duties required by this act shall be subject to suspension by the governor."[2] In practice this disciplinary power is merged in the governor's positive authority to appoint special constables.[3]

2. CENTRAL ADMINISTRATION AND CONTROL

A. Contingent

(1) APPLICABLE TO THE COMMONWEALTH IN GENERAL

In some commonwealths where simple license systems prevail, a mild power of auxiliary enforcement is given to the governor or other central administrative authority. Thus in Michigan, the general liquor law, after defining the duties of the local officers, provides that if any officer

shall willfully neglect or refuse to perform his duty under the provisions of this act, he shall be liable to a penalty of $100 for each and every offense, and the governor may, in case of such neglect or refusal, after summary hearing and determination thereon and deciding the same to have occurred, appoint such (*sic*) other person or persons to perform the duties of such officer prescribed by this act, who shall, upon being so appointed, have like powers and duties and receive the same fees . . . .[4]

The power here given to the governor could certainly be used at least to the annoyance of local officials who leave their duties undone and to the quickening of public sentiment in the matter of law-enforcement. Yet it seems to be of no practical significance. A former mayor of a Michigan

---

[1] *Ibid.*, ch. 102, § 19.   [2] *Act of* Mar. 6, 1896, § 29.

[3] See Chapter IV.   [4] *Laws of Michigan* (1895), § 2283 *d* 5.

city, a leader in prohibition party politics, writes, in answer to inquiry:

The effort to have the governor exercise his power in the matter of removing local officers derelict in their duty has not, so far as I know, been made. In one or two instances where the matter was suggested, political influences were effectual in discouraging the original movers. The whole process provided by our statutes reads well, but, under the present conditions, is practically worthless. So long as the leading political parties continue to bid against each other for the liquor vote, our statutory provision for compelling officers to do their duty will remain largely a dead letter.[1]

A distinct advance in positive central authority is found in the power of the governor to appoint special constables, in his discretion, upon proper representations showing the need of such action. The power thus enjoyed may be practically unlimited. This plan abandons the direct disciplining of the delinquent local officer, but it overwhelms him with sheer force and excludes him as a negative factor in law-enforcement. It is an engaging theory, which is presented in complete form, as applied to the enforcement of prohibition, in the Maine law of 1880, as follows:[2]

Upon petition and representation of thirty or more well known taxpayers in any county that the provisions of Chapters 17 and 27 of the Revised Statutes, and acts additional thereto and amendatory thereof, are not faithfully enforced by county and local officers, it shall be the duty of the governor and council to inquire into such representations, and if, in their judgment, such representations are well founded, the governor, by and with the consent of the council, shall appoint two or more constables for such county whose duty it shall be to diligently enforce the provisions of said chapters and acts, and for this purpose such constables shall have like powers and duties as sheriffs and deputies. For such services said constables shall receive the same compensation as is provided by law for sheriffs and deputies.

Under such authority the governor, with the coöperation

---

[1] *Letter of* Sept. 19, 1898.   [2] *Acts of* 1880, ch. 247, § 4.

of the council, may practically establish a permanent liquor
constabulary in every city, and make the force strong enough
to act independently of the local police, provided only thirty
tax-payers of the county are found faithful to the principle
of prohibition. To maintain that in any county containing a
city there are not thirty taxpayers in favor of enforcement is
to concede that the prohibitory law does not express the will
of the commonwealth. The second proposition is doubtless
true, whether the first is true or not. The prohibitory
system, although embodied in the constitution, represents a
policy, not a purpose. It is kept upon the law books through
the influence of party tradition, rural sentiment and commonwealth pride, despite the demoralizing effects of practically
licensed lawlessness in cities. The attempts made in such
cities as Bangor and Lewiston, some years ago, to enforce
the law through a county constabulary resulted in a passing
flurry and permanent failure. The failure of central authority
to enforce the law is not to be accounted for by the hostility
of local sentiment but by the fact that local sentiment is sus-
tained by the political sense of the commonwealth.

A still further advance in central authority is indicated in
the power of a commonwealth executive to appoint constables absolutely in his own discretion. This plan of administration is one of the expedients employed by South
Carolina to secure the enforcement of the dispensary law.
It is here quoted for comparison with the Maine type of
constabulary :

The governor shall have authority to appoint one or more state constables at a salary of not more than $2 per day and such expenses as
the governor may deem proper when on duty, and two chief constables at not more than $3 each per day and such expenses as the gov-
ernor may deem proper, and also one or more detectives at reasonable compensation, to see that this act is enforced, the same to be

paid from the dispensary fund in the same manner as the salary of the state commissioner.[1]

This provision has all the elements of effectiveness that such a form of administration admits. How actively it has been employed will be seen in a later chapter.[2]

(2) APPLICABLE TO CITIES IN PARTICULAR.

The peculiar difficulties attending the enforcement of restrictive legislation in cities may make it expedient to confine central administrative control to the municipal police. In order to limit central intervention to places and periods in which it is particularly needed, this type of control also may be conditionally provided, to be established and withdrawn in the discretion of the central executive. This plan of control has been considerably developed in the enforcement of prohibition in Kansas.

The contingent centralization of city police in Kansas was a part of the scheme of enforcement established just after the adoption of prohibition, nearly twenty years ago. It has been elaborated by successive acts.[3] The early laws contained a provision for the establishment of central control in a city "upon the presentation of a petition of 200 *bonâ fide* house-holders of such city, having the qualifications of electors," but such petition was not made a condition to executive action. The governor might act or refuse to act, his discretion being qualified only by the requirement that the senate approve nominees, and in later enactments the provision for petition is omitted. The hostility encountered by the commonwealth in thus invading the field formerly occupied by local authorities only resulted in more drastic legislation, extending the powers of the centrally appointed police boards and prescribing in detail the duties of munici-

---

[1] *Act of* Mar. 6, 1896, § 46.   [2] See Chapter IV.

[3] See *Kansas Gen. Statutes* (1889), § 733, etc.

palities in providing for their maintenance. These boards, which might be appointed in any of the larger cities when the interests of good government should seem to the executive council to require it, were to be composed, in each case, of three commissioners, to whom was committed the appointment of the police judge and the entire police force, as well as the complete control of the force, independently of the mayor and council. All prior public acts and all city ordinances inconsistent with the powers granted to the board were expressly abrogated. Members of such boards were made subject to removal at any time by the governor alone, who might also make appointments *ad interim*.[1]

At least five cities of Kansas have had experience with the centralized police-board system. The system, once instituted, has been maintained, apparently in the interest of the central political machine of the party in power for the time being. It seems to have been productive of no results in the interest of law-enforcement. In the city of Topeka, where prohibition sentiment is stronger than in any other city of its class, the majority of the board having shown, on one occasion, a disposition to lax enforcement, popular sentiment was evoked with a distinctness that compelled the board to do its duty.[2] In Kansas City, on the other hand, administrative efficiency is of a low order. The following quotations from a correspondent already cited, residing in Kansas City, Kansas, give, it is believed, a fair statement of the situation:

" Kansas has five cities under what we call the 'metropolitan police boards,' supposed to be non-partisan, appointed by the governor of the state. At present they are all composed of the supporters of Mr. Bryan, generally two avowed Populists and either a Democrat or a 'silver Republican' for

[1] The " metropolitan " police system in Kansas has recently been abolished.

[2] Fanshawe, *Liquor Legislation*, p. 139.

the third member.   The law was originally passed to keep
the liquor traffic out of the control of the local politicians in
the large cities, who were supposed to be selling out the
prohibitory features of the law.   It has been a failure.   (1)
The city councils would refuse to make appropriations for
the pay of the police force, and the result was a system of
fines assessed on the 'joints' each month to raise revenue.
(2) Any disregard for law always brings on others; and the
police, for a 'consideration,' would fail to report all the
'joints.'   (3) The party managers found it was a good way
to raise money for campaign purposes, and as a result only
politicians of questionable character are appointed on the
boards.   Occasionally we have had a board that seemed to
want to do its duty, and Topeka, where the temperance sentiment is strong, has nearly always had the law enforced,
but here we have hardly ever had a board that tried to do
anything but keep things going. . . . We now have just a
round hundred 'joints' which are but little better than the
open saloon." [1]

South Carolina, in 1894, added to its various administrative methods a plan of "metropolitan police," whereby a
board composed of officers of the central administration
might appoint and establish a police commission for any
large city.   The plan was applied with considerable effect in
the city of Charleston and was afterward withdrawn.   Its
operation will be considered in connection with that of the
constabulary system of South Carolina in a later chapter.[2]

B. *Definite.*

(1) APPLICABLE TO THE COMMONWEALTH IN GENERAL.

The characteristics which distinguish a definite constabulary system from a contingent one are found not so much in
the number and tenure of the force, both of which may rest in

---

[1] *Letter of* Feb. 12, 1898.   [2] See Chapter IV.

part in the discretion of the executive, as in the permanency of the organization which is worked out by statute. The typical example of a permanent constabulary is that which was developed during the prohibition era in Massachusetts.

The institution of the constabulary in Massachusetts was the logical sequel of a long period of experiments in legislative and judicial control. The original prohibitory law, of April 19th, 1838, antedating by eight years the first " Maine law," contained few administrative provisions; it was poorly enforced and was soon repealed. When prohibition was re-enacted in 1852, detailed duties were imposed upon local officers.[1] There must have been some response, for in 1854 we find an act for the protection of sheriffs and other officers in the discharge of their duties in enforcing the prohibitory law.[2] The year 1855, which marks the high tide of prohibition sentiment throughout the country, as registered on the statute books, was also the great year of administrative legislation in Massachusetts. Mayors, aldermen, selectmen and all peace officers were specifically required to arrest without warrant; prosecuting officers were hedged about with commands and incentives; neglect of duty by any officer was made punishable by a fine of $1000 and forfeiture of office; and indemnification was guaranteed to any officers mulcted in damages for acting in good faith under the prohibitory law.[3] The control of local administration was thus in large measure given over to the courts.

The legislative history of prohibition in the ensuing ten years indicates that it was a period of relaxation, following the strain of extreme activity. It seems also to have been a period of relaxation in local administration. Influences tending toward centralized police administration were at work. One of the many acts of the year 1855, relating to prohibi-

[1] *Acts of* 1852, ch. 322.   [2] *Acts of* 1854, cb. 400.
[3] *Acts of* 1855, cb. 215.

tion, began the centralization of the town agency system.[1] In his report for 1860 the commonwealth liquor commissioner complains that the agency system has no sufficient sanctions under local police administration, and in 1862 he strongly urges that a centralized police force be provided.[2]   The war intervened; yet, amid the larger issues of the time, a metropolitan police system for Boston was urged upon the legislature, chiefly to secure the enforcement of the prohibitory law.[3] One of Wendell Phillips' most powerful addresses was that of Sunday, April 5, 1863, in arraignment of the liquor tyranny of Boston.   His text was the proposition that in a city where large numbers of people and great masses of property are gathered, a police force responsible merely to the voters of the place cannot be relied upon to execute the law.   One of his sentences was prophetic of a condition that has been approximately realized in the Boston of the present day: " The moment the liquor interest of a city see that their mixing in city elections will not secure a police force in their interest, they will probably leave the election of mayor and aldermen to the natural action of ordinary politics, and then we shall have as good officers as our system will secure with the present level of education." [4]   These incidents indicated both the prevalence of illicit traffic and the trend toward centralized police administration.   The movement in favor of a "metropolitan" police system for Boston had become so strong in 1865 that it was only obviated through the introduction of a compromise measure providing a limited constabulary for service throughout the commonwealth.   It is a singular coincidence that when the friends of law enforcement were urging, in 1885, the establishment of a central police force for the commonwealth at large, the enactment of such a measure

---

[1] *Acts of* 1855, ch. 470.   [3] *Reports of " State Liquor Agent."*

[3] See *Arguments before the Joint Special Committee*, March 18, 1863:

[4] Pamphlet, Boston Public Library.

was averted by a compromise whereby a "metropolitan" police system was created for Boston alone.

The Massachusetts constabulary was at first called the "state police," and consisted of one "Constable of the Commonwealth" with at least one deputy in each county besides twenty in Suffolk (Boston), of whom not less than six must be on duty in the city at all hours.[1] Their appointment and direction was in the hands of the governor and council. They were commissioned to repress crime in general, but the reports show that their primary function was the enforcement of prohibition. In 1871 the force was reorganized under the name "constables of the commonwealth," the number was limited to seventy, and their appointment was committed to a central board of three "police commissioners." Just prior to the repeal of prohibition in 1875 the force was reduced, and, as a "state detective force," appointed by the governor and council, was assigned to general duty in aid of prosecuting officers.[2] In 1879 it gave place to the "district police,"[3] which continues as a permanent and most useful force, numbering nearly fifty.[4]

The reports of the constable of the commonwealth indicate that the constabulary in Massachusetts had substantially the same history as constabulary systems in other prohibition territory. The definiteness of its organization, however, makes its history peculiarly instructive. It began its career with the zeal of a new device. In Boston the first full year of the new régime showed 4,250 prosecutions and no less than 512 liquor dealers forced to close shop.[5] In the next year the receipts of fines and penalties recovered, as was

---

[1] *Acts of* 1865, ch. 249.   [2] *Acts of* 1875, ch. 15.

[3] *Acts of* 1879, ch. 305.

[4] See full discussion in R. H. Whitten's *Public Administration in Massachusetts*, p. 80 *ff*.

[5] *Report of the Constable of the Commonwealth*, 1866.

claimed, through the efforts of the constabulary, amounted, in the whole commonwealth, to $226,000.[1] The cost of maintenance of the force was $129,000.[1] After the first shock came the rebound. The officers of the commonwealth found arrayed against them not only the interested opposition of liquor dealers, but frequently also the undisguised hostility of local authorities; while on the part of a great body of the people there was a pronounced dissatisfaction with the invasion of the sphere of local government.[2] Fall River, for instance, refused the use of lockups to the constables.[3] Boston was willing to have the prisoner brought into the lockup, but refused to be responsible for him. When deputies appeared as prosecutors, local police officers would appear as witnesses for the defense. Upon seizure, by deputies, of liquors and appliances in illicit traffic, writs of replevin were frequently executed by local officers. Juries of the vicinage generally refused to convict. Two courses were open whereby to stop this internecine strife within the administration. One was to repeal the prohibitory law; the other, to strengthen the constabulary with new rules of judicial procedure. Both courses were followed, in succession. Prohibition was swept away in 1868, being replaced with low license and local option;[4] a year later, by a resurgence of puritan sentiment, it was carried to a higher point than before.[5] For the first six months under the new law, the constable of the commonwealth reported: Number of dealers in the commonwealth, 5,523; prosecutions, 1,676; convictions, 1,404; fines recovered, $178,962.

---

[1] *Ibid.*, 1867.   [2] *Ibid., passim.*

[3] *Reports of the Constable of the Commonwealth.* The attitude of the commonwealth toward the national administration's enforcement of the Fugitive Slave Law in 1851 is an interesting historic parallel. See Burgess' *The Middle Period*, p. 370; and *cf.* Chapter V, on replevins in South Carolina.

[4] *Acts of* 1868, ch. 141.   [5] *Acts of* 1869, ch. 415.

Some succeeding years showed larger nominal results, but from this time on until its final repeal in 1875 the prohibitory law was weakened by successive amendments, resulting in increasing difficulties of enforcement. In 1870 the force numbered nearly two hundred. In his report for 1870 the constable complains of the wide-spread abuse of the ale-and-beer law, especially in the matter of Sunday sales; and in 1871 he concludes that on account of relaxations in the law, in spite of police efforts, "the traffic is not materially checked."

The failure of the constabulary to enforce prohibition, in Massachusetts as in other commonwealths, thus seems to have been due to the fact that the people, when put to the test, did not want the law enforced. Local sentiment might have impeded but it could not persistently have prevented centralized enforcement. It is the common sense of the commonwealth that controls. The continuance and the eminently useful services[1] of the centralized "district police," in promoting the enforcement of laws that meet with the general approval of the body politic, show that there is a place for such a police force; they vindicate the wisdom of the words of Governor Andrews in his valedictory to the legislature of 1866: "The maintenance of such a civil force, directly responsible to the chief executive magistrate, is of high importance and will yet prove essential to the commonwealth."

Maine copied the Massachusetts constabulary plan, with modifications, in 1867, but abandoned it in the following year.[2]

(2) APPLICABLE TO CITIES IN PARTICULAR
(a) Earlier Period

Central control of metropolitan police was an idea im-

[1] Whitten, *op. cit.*, p. 88 *ff.*   [2] *The Liquor Problem*, p. 27.

ported from England. By act of Parliament of June 19,
1829, there was created about the city of London a "Metropolitan Police District," to be under the supervision, for
police administration, of two Justices of the Peace, specially
designated for the purpose by the crown.[1]   The plan was
variously elaborated, and in 1856 a single commissioner, with
two assistant commissioners, was placed at the head of the
metropolitan police, who were under the general control of
the Home Secretary.[2]   The plan was designed primarily to
secure unity of police administration throughout a thickly
settled district which it was not deemed expedient to con-
solidate for all purposes.   It was evidently intended also to
supply an efficient administration where local administration
had proved inefficient.[3]

The earlier imitations of the English pattern in the United
States are chiefly of interest as showing the beginnings and
development of a plan which has since assumed great significance.   Except in probibition territory, the establishment
of the early metropolitan police boards seems not to have
been especially connected with the problems of liquor law administration.   We have seen, however, that the metropolitan
excise board of New York city grew, in part, out of the
metropolitan police board.   It is also worth noting that in
1855, only two years before the creation of this board, the
legislature of New York had enacted a drastic prohibitory
law, which lingered for two years, un-enforced.   It was a
period of ethical agitation.   Prohibition and abolition senti-
ments were rife.   When put in positive, statutory form both
alike stirred up strife which necessitated repressive administration.   The cumulative force of ethical motives and partisan
zeal in the political action of the period led to the working
out of rigorous measures for police enforcement.

[1] 10 *Geo. IV*, 225.   [2] *Cf*. Maitland's *Justice and Police.*

[3] The general act for an improved constabulary under central supervision was
passed in the same year, 1856. *Cf*. Maltbie, *op. cit.*

New York instituted a metropolitan system in 1857.[1] The police department of New York city, as an organized branch of its municipal administration, had been in existence hardly more than a quarter of a century.   At this time, however, it was already organized on a modern basis and was under the general control of the mayor.   The act of 1857 threw into one metropolitan police district New York city, Brooklyn and adjacent territory to an extent approximating the present limits of " greater New York." Five resident commissioners appointed for three-year terms by the governor, with the concurrence of the senate, together with the mayors of New York city and Brooklyn respectively, constituted the "board of metropolitan police."   Besides giving them the usual and complete powers of a police board, the act specially enjoined upon them the enforcement of the laws against gambling, and against the sale of liquors on election days and Sundays.

Subsequent legislation increased the powers of the board. In 1860 the original law was modified and re-enacted in seventy sections; the mayors were now excluded, the numbers of commissioners reduced to three, and the term extended to six years.[2]   Again, in 1864, the three commissioners were legislated out of office, four commissioners were named by the legislature and the term was fixed at eight years, while distrust of the executive was further manifested in the provision that vacancies occurring during a recess of the legislature should be filled by the remaining commissioners.[3]   A metropolitan sanitary district, a metropolitan board of health, a metropolitan fire department, a special bureau of elections and other centralized commissions seem to have left the city authorities free to devote their attention to "public works" and private profits.   The metropolitan system of centralization was abolished in 1870.

[1] *Act of* Apr. 15, 1857; ch. 569.   [2] *Laws of* 1860, ch. 259.
[3] *Laws of* 1864, cb. 41.

The example of New York was followed by several other commonwealths, with various modifications. In 1860 Maryland provided for the city of Baltimore a police board, to consist of the mayor, *ex officio*, and four commissioners selected by the legislature on joint ballot.[1] In 1862 the number of commissioners was reduced to three; still later, the mayor was excluded, the board continuing, as at present, with three commissioners elected by the legislature, one every two years, for a six-year term. As usual, in such systems, the city council is required to provide for the expenses of the department on requisition of the board; a somewhat unusual and apparently effective sanction is supplied in the power, given to the board, to provide for deficiencies by issuing certificates of debt which shall be valid against the city.[2] This system, it will be observed, is one rather of legislative than of administrative control. There is said to be a strong sentiment among the citizens in favor of the transfer of the power of appointment to the governor.

The plan of direct administrative control was adopted by Missouri, which instituted, at the same period,[3] a " metropolitan" police for St. Louis. The control of the police was given to a board consisting of the mayor, *ex officio*, and four commissioners to be appointed by the governor, the act providing that the police organization should be entirely independent of the city government.[4] The home-made charter ratified by the voters of the city in 1876 embodied this plan of police, which has continued substantially unchanged. Both St. Louis and Baltimore are under license laws. Both have centralized license commissions separate from the police boards. In recent years the enforcement of repressive liquor

---

[1] *Laws of* 1860, ch. 7.

[2] T. P. Thomas, " *The City Government of Baltimore*," *J. H. U. Studies*, XIV.

[3] 1861.

[4] M. S. Snow, " *The City Government of St. Louis*," *J. H. U. Studies*, V.

laws seems to have been, in both cities, more efficient than could reasonably have been expected from a local police management. It is generally admitted that the Sunday-closing law is not enforced in St. Louis; but good order is maintained, and even those who oppose the theory have "no severe criticism" for the plan in practice.[1]

The Detroit police board, established in 1865,[2] is an instance of the early employment of the metropolitan plan in a prohibition commonwealth. The prohibition element seems, however, to have had no controlling influence in the establishment of the system. In the same year the creation by the New York legislature of the "capital police district," with a centrally appointive board of police, including in its jurisdiction the city of Albany and some adjacent territory,[3] indicated a tendency to apply the metropolitan plan to smaller cities. A similar act, creating the "Rensselaer police district," to include the city of Troy,[4] led to the overthrow of the policy by the courts.[5] A succession of judicial decisions on the various metropolitan acts in different commonwealths had established the general doctrine of the ample power of the legislature, unless clearly inhibited by the constitution, to vest the control of municipal police in the central administration.[6] The court now held, however, that such acts of the legislature should be justified by their intrinsic expediency, and that the terms of the act might be examined by the court to determine the true motives leading

---

[1] Albert Shaw, in the *Century*, June, 1896. See also *The Liquor Problem*, p. 336.

[2] *Act of* Feb. 28, 1865.   [3] *Laws of* 1865, ch. 554.

[4] *Laws of* 1873, ch. 638.   [5] People *v.* Albertson, 55 *N. Y.*, 50.

[6] People *v.* Draper, 15 *N. Y.*, 532—(1857). Mayor *v.* State, 15 *Md.*, 376—(1860). People *v.* Mahaney, 13 *Mich.*, 481—(1865). People *v.* Shepard, 36 *N. Y.*, 285—(1866). See especially Judge Cooley's philosophic discussion of rights of local government in People *v.* Hurlbut, 24 *Mich.*, 44. For present-day facts *cf. Municipal Affairs*, Dec., 1898.

to its enactment; upon technical grounds, supported by such considerations of public policy, this act was declared unconstitutional. A similar judicial policy has been followed, as we have seen, in respect to metropolitan police acts of a more recent date in the west.[1] The decision in the Rensselaer case may be taken, however, as closing the first experimental period of metropolitan police administration. In so far as it had not been dictated by considerations of partisan advantage, the early development of the idea might be described as a blind groping after improvement in municipal police administration generally. Its subsequent development is somewhat more particularly connected with liquor legislation.

(b) *Later Period.*

The first period of aggressive temperance sentiment in the United States reached its moral culmination in the total abstinence movement of the '40's, and crystallized in the prohibitory laws of the '50's. As we have seen, a considerable development of centralized police administration followed. The second marked period of temperance agitation began with the women's crusade of moral suasion against the saloon in the early '70's, and left its legal record in the multitude of restrictive laws of that and the following decade. Prohibitory laws were enacted in a number of commonwealths, especially in the middle west, beginning with Kansas in 1880; the record of prohibitory enactments for that decade being second only to the record of the decade following 1850. The east had learned by experience that general prohibitory laws were, as yet, impossible of enforcement, but stringent license laws were generally enacted, accompanied in most cases with provision for local option on the question of prohibition.

Local option meant generally a large measure of rural

[1] See Chapter II.

prohibition. The rural problem in its essential features therefore remained practically the same as under general prohibition; and the rural problem has never been the troublesome one in the administration of liquor laws. In the cities, on the other hand, the general introduction of a rational license policy in place of an impossible prohibitory one has been accompanied with a rational demand for the enforcement of regulations. In some instances the commonwealth has adopted a still more liberal policy, in removing the restraints of a license system, as in New York. Here the need as well as the justice of maintaining strict enforcement of measures for the repression of the evils attending the traffic is still more strongly emphasized. Centralized administrative control of municipal police, where it is found to-day, is thus vitally related to the liquor problem, and may be regarded as in part the administrative sequel of the restrictive liquor legislation of this later period.

A very mild form of control, both in its organization and in its operation, is that in which a centrally appointed commission serves as advisory council to the executive head of the municipal police department. Such a system was instituted for Cincinnati in 1886, four commissioners appointed by the governor having authority to negative police appointments proposed by the mayor.[1] Two years before, a prohibitory amendment to the constitution had received, apparently, a majority of the popular vote but, as its friends claimed, was "counted out." The police force of Cincinnati has a high reputation for physical efficiency; but no serious pretense is made of enforcing the liquor laws. The Sunday-closing law, especially, has long been looked upon as a dead letter in that city. It should be noticed however, that the usual antecedents of administrative control of police are want-

[1] *Report of National Conference for Good City Government*, 1895.

ing in Ohio.   In the first place, license being forbidden by the constitution, the primary administration of the law involves nothing but the collection of the tax; restrictive administration is thus minimized.   In the second place, legislative regulation has not extended to great detail, municipalities being given "full power to regulate, restrain and prohibit" the traffic.[1]

The extreme of extension in applying the principle of city police centralization has recently been illustrated in Indiana. Two years ago the Secretary of State wrote: " It is an established principle in Indiana that the police regulations of the state shall be executed by local administration, and we discover no tendency to disturb this principle."[2]   The conditions discoverable in 1898 are described by the same official as follows:[3]

Under what is known as the Metropolitan Police Law of this State, each city of ten thousand or over has a police board, appointed by the Governor of the State.   The board consists of three police commissioners, one whom must be of opposite political faith from that of the other two.   This board appoints a chief of police and the subordinate officers and the patrolmen.   Under the law the members of the force are divided equally between the leading political parties. The police commissioners and police departments under them have no special powers conferred with reference to the enforcement of the liquor law.   They take an oath to enforce all law, which includes the liquor law.   As a matter of fact, however, the desire of the Board of Police Commissioners is followed with reference to the enforcement of the liquor law as well as other laws.   If the board wants a lax administration, a lax administration it is.   If the board seeks a thorough enforcement, it is easily obtained.   In some cities, the letter of the law is enforced.   In other cities the law is a dead letter, all depending upon the will of the Board of Police Commissioners.

---

[1] *" Dow law," as amended*, Feb. 20, 1896.

[2] *Letter of* Dec. 21, 1896.   [3] *Letter of* Sept. 19, 1898.

The enforcement of prohibition in cities through a permantly centralized police administration has recently been put to the test in New Hampshire. Police commissions appointed by the governor and council have been established in some of the larger cities, including Manchester and Concord. It can hardly be presumed that the system was instituted with the expectation that the prohibitory law would be enforced through it. The prohibitory law of New Hampshire is the weakest law to be found on the subject in any of the commonwealths: in permitting the manufacture while forbidding the sale of liquors it invites violations. The sentiment in support of the law, too, as shown by legislative votes on the question of repeal, is weakening from year to year. The following words, although written by an ardent prohibitionist, describe a situation which might logically be expected: "I can see that with a governor and council who would regard their solemn oath of office the system might be a very great improvement upon the old system; but as things are here in New Hampshire, the police commissioners are a fraud and a defence to law-breakers. In nearly every city of this prohibition state where police commissions control the police force they have permitted the establishment of a practical license system, and the governor and council refuse to turn them out of office."[1]

Centralization of city police administration, when conjoined with license administration, has already been considered.[2] The positive activity of the Boston police force in the repression of crime as well as in its other service auxilliary to the license administration has been described. The principal objections to the Boston plan arise from its comprehensiveness. The police powers of the board are, in practice, thorough-going and tend to become more and

---

[1] *Letter of* Feb. 8, 1899.   [2] See Chapter II.

more extensive through additional legislation. Besides having complete charge of the general police force the board controls the park police, the "street police," the harbor police and an extensive ambulance service. It is also charged with the administration of licenses in general, such as those for hackney carriages, "public lodging houses," common victuallers, itinerant musicians and street-railway conductors and drivers. By a recent act the board is further authorized to appoint " railroad police," and may also, upon the written application of any officer or board in charge of a department in the city of Boston, approved by the mayor of said city, appoint special police officers for such department.[1] Provision is also made in this act for persons in the employ of private parties to be commissioned by the board as special officers. These specimen provisions are given to show into what extensive details the powers of the board have been carried. These functions far transcend the province claimed by the defenders of central administration as belonging to it in theory. Such extensions of authority are due to considerations of administrative convenience—not to the moral necessity which justified the establishment of the system. They tend to involve the central board in the wheels of local machinery to such an extent as to make it difficult to preserve the harmony of municipal government.

We have seen how intimately the work of the Boston police force is involved in the efficient enforcement of the restrictive license laws.[2] In their general duty of preserving the peace and order of the community it is impossible to divide the work of the police officers on the lines of the enforcement of liquor laws. There is no reason for a strict division, if it were possible. What would seem to be desirable and practicable is the differentiation of those branches of administration which are distinctively the func-

---

[1] *Acts of* 1898, ch. 282.　　　　[2] *Cf.* Chapter II.

tion of peace officers from those which are not. The peace functions would naturally fall to the police and license board, and may be suitable subjects of centralized administration. Other regulative functions could be given over to local authorities. The highly specialized organization of municipal administration in Boston would, it is believed, make possible such a distribution of functions without loss of energy or sacrifice of unity.[1]

II. *Theory*

The correlative of license as a legislative policy is prohibition. The correlative of permission, as an administrative process, is repression. In so far as license implies restraint, it takes on the character of prohibition and puts upon the administration the duty of repression. It has been difficult, in discussing license administration, to avoid mixing it with police administration in the narrow sense, simply because license, involving restriction, calls into play the repressive action of the administration. It may be highly advantageous to an efficient enforcement of the "conditions of license" that the license authority be closely associated with the police authority. But when the licensing function has been once exercised as respects a particular person or place, the license authority proper becomes *functus officio* for that case; the enforcement of attendant prohibitions is a matter of penal administration. Where there is no license required, but various conditions precedent are imposed, the case is not essentially changed. The exaction of a tax as a condition precedent similarly subjects those doing business without prior payment to the repressive action of the administration. The New York Court of Appeals, in construing the Liquor Tax law of 1896, says: "All exactions imposed

---

[1] *Cf.* "*The Present Scope of Government,*" Eugene Wambaugh, *Atlantic Monthly,* Jan., 1898.

upon citizens by public authority are in a general sense taxes, whether imposed for regulation or revenue;" but the court holds that the law in question was enacted under the police powers of the commonwealth, and adds: "The payment of the tax and the giving of a bond are conditions precedent to the right to engage in the business, and the imposition of conditions precedent is the distinguishing test of a license law." [1]

One difference between permissive laws and prohibitory laws is that the permissive policy is one of "hands off" as respects the consumer. The right to drink is not infringed. Excepting certain classes, such as minors, Indians and habitual drunkards, every man can drink to intoxication without violation of the conditions of the permit by anybody. When, having become "an intoxicated person," he is no longer a legal vendee, he is bundled out upon the side-walk and becomes the object of the general repressive action of the administration in the interest of the peace and order of the community. If his drams have left him in a stupor he must be removed from the street as an object offensive to the public sense of decency. If the effect of alcohol upon the brain has been to relax the inhibitions of self-control upon jovial impulses, he may have to be suppressed as a living nuisance for disturbing the quiet of the night. If, again, his impulses thus turned loose are violent, he may have to be taken under the restraint of the state for assult or homicide. All such activity of the administration, however, is quite apart from the enforcement of license laws proper; it is general enforcement of peace and order.

A simple license policy, under which opportunities to drink are not seriously curtailed, thus encounters, in its enforcement, only the opposition of the avarice which desires freedom to sell. As restrictions are added, however, whether

---

[1] People *ex. rel.* Einsfeld *v.* Murray, 149 *N. Y.*, 367.

through increased tax or through detailed police regulations, not only does the desire for gain through trade impel to violations of the law but the freedom of the individual to buy as he pleases and drink what he wants is more or less hampered.   Restrictions imposed upon dealers thus become prohibitions which bear upon the people generally and en- counter corresponding resistance.   Prohibition may be either local or temporal.   A Sunday-closing law is a temporal pro- hibitory law.   If there is a wide-spread demand for liquor on Sunday, such a law will call for a corresponding exercise of repressive administration.   Night-closing induces similar op- position and necessitates similar repressive enforcement, which, however, may be of less significance on account of the smaller number who are affected by such restrictions.   The imposition of a high license tax may, by reducing the number of saloons, make them less conveniently accessible to certain neighborhoods.   The interdiction of music in drinking-places may be grievous to some customers.   Every step thus taken to limit the indulgence of his tastes by the individual is a step in the direction of prohibition.   The social significance of prohibition is that the state stands between the individual and the satisfaction of his desires.   Its administrative sig- nificance is that it requires a degree of repressive activity corresponding to the aggregate force of the desires which have been outlawed.   The latest and most notable method of regulation attempts to restrict the evils of drink by elim- inating the social feature of the open traffic. This expedient runs counter to an instinct so strong as to call for a high degree of repressive activity on the part of the administra- tion.   The sorts of restriction just mentioned may be re- garded as instances of a third class, which, as distinguished from local and temporal prohibition, may be described as modal prohibition.

The crux of the liquor problem is the reconciling of police

regulation with sumptuary and social desires.   Over against
the ethical principle in legislation is set the social principle in
human nature; over against economic welfare is set physical
appetite; over against the functions of government are set
the instincts of personal liberty,—and the conflict is more
acute and more far-reaching than in most of the spheres of
human interest which government has entered.   The problem involves a touch of nature which makes most men kin.
Repressive administration of liquor laws is therefore peculiarly concerned with that product of the social mind which
we call public opinion, or the general sentiment of the community.

The effect of public sentiment upon the efficiency of a
local administration may be represented in the form of a
ratio, thus: [1]

$$\text{Local administrative efficiency} = \frac{\text{Local sentiment}}{\text{Legislative requirement}}$$

This equation is to be taken as true only under the simplified conditions, other factors than public sentiment being excluded.   The problem is the improvement of the local administrative efficiency.   This will approach perfection as local sentiment approaches the standard of legislative requirement.   The
officers whose efficiency is in question here are presumed to
be responsible directly or indirectly to the local electorate,
and local sentiment is taken to be the consensus of the constituent community.

Legislative requirement being normally the expression of
the average political and moral sense of the body politic, it may
frequently happen that local sentiment is already in advance
of the legal norm.   Such a case is outside the present problem.   It emphasizes the propriety of the local option policy

---

[1] Using a form suggested by James, *Psychology*, ch. X, following Carlyle, *Sartor
Resartus*, ch. IX.

whereby the surplus moral force of the community, instead of going to waste, may impose such special and local restrictions as it is able to enforce. Complete and general prohibition, being in theory absolute, is the only condition in which local sentiment cannot possibly exceed the requirements of the law. In practice, however, only a few communities will be found, and those the less thickly settled, in which some means will not have to be sought to improve the efficiency of local administration, under any system of legislative regulation that pretends to be restrictive.

Let us assume that local sentiment is below the legislative standard: it is evident, from the nature of the ratio, that its value may be increased either by increasing its first term or by diminishing its second term. The standard of local sentiment may be raised by the slow process of education, in which written laws have their part. There may also be cataclysmic changes, as when a wave of moral sentiment sweeps over a country at a period when for some reason the public mind is peculiarly susceptible. Such movements, however, unless they amount to a revolution, are usually followed by a reaction in which the results gained are mostly lost, except for their educational value. In lieu of satisfactory elevation of local sentiment, resort may be had to the other natural method of establishing equilibrium, the lowering of the standards embodied in the law.

To lower the requirements of a law in order to secure efficiency in the enforcement of it is a natural expedient at least in the sense that such a policy persisted in would reduce political society to a state of nature. The ideal of political action is a leveling up. Democracy must give effect to the will of the people; but unless it include a measure of aristocracy it is likely to end in anarchy. The civilization of the national state is better than that of the village community partly because of the upward pull that the organic whole exerts upon the weaker parts. Men cannot be made good by law; but a good law, well enforced, helps to keep men good and make them better. If a particular locality is below the general standard in enforcement, outside assistance may prepare the way for self-help.

The introduction of central control as an element in local administrative efficiency gives rise to relations which may be represented in the form of a ratio as follows:

$$\text{Centralized administrative efficiency} = \frac{\text{General sentiment}}{\text{Legislative requirement}}$$

This formula, like the other, is true not as a general proposition but only as regards the relations of the terms with which it is concerned. Moreover, since administration must be local in action, notwithstanding it is under central responsibility, the actual intensity of general sentiment at a particular place is diminished more or less by the remoteness of some parts of the general body politic. The sentiment of the local community thus has, in practice, a disproportionate effect in the make-up of general sentiment. If, therefore, general sentiment be not strong and pronounced in favor of the enforcement of the law as laid down by the legislature, centralized administration is likely to weaken and fail in the face of an aggressive local opposition. So long as general sentiment, which, normally, is on a par with central legislative requirement, is intense enough to carry the administration against the force of local sentiment, the conditions are favorable to the efficiency of centralized administrative control.

The activities of the public mind are peculiarly quickened by social contact and reaction in cities. The conditions of life and work for a large portion of the population of the great city are unfavorable to normal restraints of physical appetite. Social instincts unite with physical appetites to produce an association out of which grow a stronger desire and demand for freedom in the gratification of these instincts and appetites. It is doubtful if the various processes of education, with their conservative influence, keep pace with this progressive development of liberalism in cities, which is promoted by the constant accession of new elements from without and from the higher social classes to the lower. At any rate, the present tendency seems to be toward more liberal city standards in the matter of liquor regulations. If, in such a case, the legislative judgment of the commonwealth insists that the general laws shall be maintained, the only general expedient for securing their enforcement in cities is centralized control of police.

Central administrative control of police has, as we have seen, been provided on one of two general plans: contingent, or definite. Theoretically, a contingent scheme of centralized control of city police, to be assumed and put into effect by the executive when conditions require it, is most conducive to immediate efficiency. It should also contribute to permanent improvement, through the discipline administered to the municipality. In practice, the wholesome exercise of such a power, when it involves the setting up of his own appointees by the governor, calls for wisdom, integrity and courage in a degree in which few governors possess these qualities. It is difficult for a man who has been elected governor of one of our commonwealths to free himself from partisan and personal obligations far enough to appoint good men to existing offices. When he is empowered not only to appoint local officers but first to create the offices, in his discretion, his temptations are multiplied. In creating a " metropolitan " police board the executive must, as a rule, act either in accordance with the wish of law-abiding citizens and in defiance of the dominant element in local politics, or in compliance with the demands of place-hunters who urge intervention for their own aggrandizement. The creation of such boards by definite legislation, on the other hand, although liable to similar abuse, is at least the act of a deliberative body in which the force of personal motives is weakened on account of numbers. Moreover, the interval between sessions of the legislature, even if the sessions be biennial, is not too long to allow for events to demonstrate the need of central intervention if it goes to the extent of a reorganization of police control. The displacement of local police management by a centralized management permanently or for an indefinite period is properly a legislative function, and its surrender to the executive should be viewed with suspicion. Finally, assuming the honest intent of the executive head of the commonwealth, he cannot represent so certainly as the legislature that consensus of public opinion upon which the efficiency of centralized administration depends.

Definitely centralized control affords a basis for sympathetic coöperation between the people and the police. The infinite diversity of interests committed to police guardianship, the wide variety of ways in which the legitimate objects of police administration may be pursued, the peculiar efficacy of tactful methods and complaisant manners in winning the coöperation of the people, the effect of the attitude of the public upon the *morale* of the force, all these factors of the problem of police administration emphasize the importance of a well-considered, harmonious plan of organization. The element of permanency supplied by wise and definite legislation permits the people to accommodate their political interest to an imported institution; while an effective central executive control can keep the administration from becoming demoralized by local influences. How to secure wise and disinterested legislation and how to insure upright and energetic administrative control is a problem for the moralist. All that political science can do is to throw around these functions such safeguards of administrative legislation as experience has proved valuable.   When a wise plan of control has been established and an enlightened policy of administration has been instituted, the results must rest ultimately with that general sense of right throughout the body politic which, as it makes law, also enforces it.

CHAPTER IV

COMMERCIAL ADMINISTRATION

I *Development*

THE TOWN AGENCY UNDER PROHIBITION

THE economic activity of the commonwealth in engaging in the liquor traffic is closely connected both in theory and in practice with prohibition. The dispensary system and the prohibitory régime agree in forbidding traffic for private profit. Sometimes prohibition permits private traffic for specified purposes, as, for instance, sales by druggists for use as medicine or in the arts. From the point of view of the theory of free trade such prohibition is less prohibitory than the dispensary system. In practice, however, prohibition has frequently been associated with the actual management of such limited traffic by the government.

The town agency system appeared with the beginnings of prohibition. The Massachusetts act of April 19, 1838, which prohibited the retail trade in spirituous liquors, permitted, it is true, the limited traffic by apothecaries, but required that they be licensed for this business by the same boards which had formerly granted licenses under the general license law. Upon the renewal of prohibition in 1852, the town agency system was formally inaugurated, under local control. The appointment of town agents and the management of agencies was committed to the selectmen, who were required to report to the county commissioners.[1] Gradually legislative regulations accumulated, bonds, records and other formalities being pre-

---

[1] *Acts of* 1852, ch. 322.

scribed.[1] In 1855 the office of " state commissioner" was
created, to be filled by appointment of the governor and
council.[2] The commissioner, however, was rather an agent
than an officer of the commonwealth, yet he was given
peculiar powers and subjected to special obligations. He
received no salary, provided his own capital and could contract no liabilities as against the commonwealth. He was
given the monopoly of the wholesale trade with town agents,
and his seal was made the sole passport for liquors in transit.
He was limited to a net profit of 5 per cent. on sales and was
required to keep his books open to inspection by the prosecuting officers of the commonwealth. The centralized administration thus inchoately organized was extended by its
own interested activity. The term of the commissioner was
fixed, regular reports were required, and he was even allowed
to enter the field of retail trade by appointing a limited number of sub-agents in Boston.[3] This direct centralization of
traffic was evidently an expedient of " back-firing" to help
kill the illicit trade which local authorities failed to suppress.

The reports of the Massachusetts liquor commissioner,
even in the earlier stage of the development of the office,
show a *quasi*-governmental enterprise similar in character
though not in extent to that of the South Carolina dispensary.[4] For the year 1859, sales to local agents amounted to
$123,626. In 1860 the commissioner had dealings with 259
of the 335 towns, and recommended in his report that he be
authorized to appoint agents in towns refusing to maintain
agencies. He also looked abroad for trade. Having been
given permission by the legislature to sell to authorized
agents in neighboring prohibition commonwealths, he published his readiness " to meet all demands, ... also to

---

[1] *Acts of* 1855, ch. 215.   [2] *Acts of* 1855, ch. 470.

[3] *Acts of* 1858, ch. 172.

[4] See *Reports*, 1858 to 1865, *of Commonwealth Liquor Commissioner*.

offer proper inducements, ... having on hand about 130 different kinds and grades of wines and liquors and in amount an average of $30,000 of stock, ... at prices which defy legal competion." This amounted, as the commissioner aptly remarks, to "a retail trade." He secured the patronage of Maine, New Hampshire and Vermont, with the result of increased sales and larger gains. Another advantage resulting from this enterprise was the absorption by the commonwealth's commissioner of an interstate commerce which was formerly in private hands, and hence was likely to be productive of illicit traffic at home. The system, in general, projected the element of private gain into a plan of police regulation, with the inevitable result, observable also in the dispensary system, that the motive of gain tended to obscure the police purpose of the system. That the enterprise of the commisioner got the better of his ideals of official duty was strongly indicated by his refusal, in a notable instance, to permit legislative inquest into his accounts.[1] The report for 1862, another person having become commissioner, likewise indicates a strange commercial competition for a prohibited traffic. It says: "The people have traded with the agents to a greater extent than formerly, showing either an increased necessity for these articles or a growing suspicion of the quality of those obtained from other sources."

With the re-enactment of prohibition in 1869, after a year of "license," the agency system, like the constabulary, reappeared more thoroughly organized than before. The commissioner was now made a salaried officer, at $4000 per year; the "state assayer" was also given a regular salary.[2] In 1871, after the decadence of prohibition sentiment had been signalized by the passage of the "ale and beer" law, permitting the sale of such liquors to be consumed off the

[1] Burnham *v.* Morrissey, 14 *Gray*, 226.

[2] *Acts of* 1869, ch. 415.

premises,[1] the commercial character of the commonwealth's traffic was still further emphasized. The commissioner was allowed to enter this general traffic, at least in Boston, through sub-agents appointed by him; and it was provided that " All profits accruing from such sales shall be paid into the treasury of the commonwealth."[2]

Prohibition in New England has generally been accompanied with the town-agency system, under varying forms of control. Vermont formerly had a central commissioner who enjoyed summary powers of control over town agents, but more recently the control of town agencies was given to an elective county commissioner.[3] New Hampshire organized the agencies as early as 1858, in an act which has been perpetuated in part as follows: " The governor shall from time to time appoint one or more suitable persons " to furnish town agents with " pure, unadulterated, spirituous liquors, on such terms and under such regulations and restrictions as to him may seem proper."[4] Maine established the office of " state dispensing commissioner " in 1862, to be filled by appointment of the governor and council. His duties, as defined by a more recent act, are chiefly ministerial, the commonwealth being the virtual purchaser of liquors to be furnished by the commissioner to town agencies. Although the commissioner provides the capital with which to carry on the business, he can hardly be regarded as the entrepreneur. He receives a prescribed rate of interest on the capital invested, as well as a salary of $1500, and expenses, for his services as manager of the commonwealth's traffic. He is appointed for a four-year term, makes his headquarters " at such place as shall be approved by the governor and council" and is under their general supervision and direction.[5] Maine

[1] *Acts of* 1870, ch. 389.   [2] *Acts of* 1871, ch. 374.
[3] *Statutes of Vt.* (1894.)   [4] *Public Laws of N. H.* (1891), ch. 112.
[5] *Acts of* 1887, ch. 140, *as amended*, 1895, ch. 160.

has thus reached not only the stage of administrative development at which Massachusetts stopped, but, so far as the traffic extends, she has practically the plan of control, by governor and council, with which South Carolina began. An expansion of the field of governmental enterprise, with an attendant elaboration of administrative organization, changes the prohibitory-agency system into the commonwealth dispensary. Although, in the important types of the agency system, the central commissioner has no direct control over local agents, a considerable supervisory authority may be exercised by the central administration. The Maine law of 1895 requires the governor and council to inspect local agencies once a year in towns, twice a year in cities, and at any other time on complaint of municipal officers.

II. *Current Form*

THE COMMONWEALTH DISPENSARY

The establishment of the commonwealth dispensary system in South Carolina was a sufficiently new and marked departure from previous systems to be called a revolution. Its subsequent existence has been a progressive evolution. From the first, it has carried into the realm of central governmental activity a degree of commercial and police administration which had not been approached in any previous plan of dealing with the liquor traffic. The policy of the South in liquor legislation was to have no distinctive policy except that of legislating specially for different localities. It is perhaps due to this policy or absence of policy that the idea of the dispensary was suggested to South Carolina. The Georgia legislature, which, at its session of 1889, had enacted between seventy and eighty special liquor laws for as many separate localities,[1] indulged the city of Athens, at its next

---

[1] See *Session Laws*, 1889.

session, with a local dispensary system which is said to have been the model for South Carolina.[1] The first commonwealth dispensary act, that of South Carolina, which went into effect July 1, 1893, was described in its title as "An act to prohibit the manufacture and sale of intoxicating liquors, as a beverage, within this state, except as herein provided." In 1896 it had become:

An act to provide for the election of a state board of control and to further regulate the sale, use, consumption, transportation, and disposition of intoxicating or alcoholic liquors or liquids in the state, and prescribe further penalties for violation of the dispensary laws, and to police the same.

The repressive character of the law and the wide administrative activities which it requires have kept it constantly before the courts. It has been picked to pieces repeatedly by the courts and its essential parts condemned as unconstitutional, but it has never failed to appear in new and stronger form after the next meeting of the legislature. The controversy generally hinged upon the question whether the law was a police measure or a revenue measure. The decisions on this question will be considered hereafter. It will be convenient to disregard for the present the final motive of the act and to treat the dispensary merely as a governmental monopoly of the liquor traffic, involving primarily a business administration and, secondarily, an incidental, repressive, police administration. In describing the organization of the system, the dispensary law as revised and re-enacted March 6, 1896, will generally be followed.

I. BUSINESS ADMINISTRATION

(1) ORGANIZATION

The law as originally framed, under the inspiration of a strong and aggressive personality in the executive chair, gave

---

[1] *Act of* Aug. 31, 1891.

the general direction of the dispensary to a board of control consisting of the governor, the comptroller-general and the attorney-general. The executive management of the system was committed to a central dispensary commissioner appointed by the governor. Later, the legislature assumed the appointment of the board of control, which consists of five members chosen for five-year terms.[1] This board appoints the central commissioner and the several county boards of control, besides appointing assistant chemists and the necessary force of clerks and fixing the salaries of these subordinate officers. Its appointing power is qualified by the proviso that all appointees must be "believed by the said board not to be addicted to the use of intoxicating liquors." All its appointees are removable for cause in the discretion of the board. The compensation of the members of the board is a *per diem* allowance and mileage equal to that of members of the legislature.

All liquors to be sold within the commonwealth must be purchased by the central board of control and furnished through the dispensary to local dispensers or other authorized vendors. The certificate of the board and that of the official chemist must be attached to every package of liquors in commercial transit.[2] The manufacture of liquors within the commonwealth and their shipment for external trade is forbidden except under license from the board of control.[3] Managers of distilleries are required to make regular reports, showing the disposition of the product, the board appointing a special inspector to keep manufacturers under surveillance.[4] The law formerly required that preference be given to producers within the commonwealth, but in consequence of the rulings of the federal courts against this discrimination it was

[1] *Act of* March 6, 1896; § 2.

[2] *Ibid.*, § 3.   [3] *Ibid.*, § 15.   [4] *Ibid.*

repealed and the board of control was left free to buy liquors where it could do so most advantageously.

The central board of control has wide discretion. Its supplementary ordinance power extends to prescribing " all rules and regulations governing the said commissioner or county dispensers . . . . where the same are not provided for by law." [1] Exemption from the general prohibition upon the sale of liquors by any person other than dispensers may be granted by the board in the case of qualified hotels "where tourists or health-seekers resort," bond having first been given in the penal sum of $3,000 that all rules will be observed and no liquors sold except those procured from the dispensary.[2] The board, under stress of adverse rulings by the courts, has also extended its activity beyond the limits prescribed in the law and even against the manifest disapproval of the legislature, in establishing "beer dispensaries," to contest the field with the private traffic which flourished for a time in the shape of "original packages." All expenses of the central dispensary management are paid upon warrants drawn by the board upon the commonwealth treasurer, who keeps a separate account with the dispensary fund.

The central commissioner holds for a two-year term on a salary of $1900 per annum, resides at the capital, and acts in general as business manager under the direction of the board of control. As the central dispensing agent he supplies local dispensaries with "merchandise" for the retail trade and also deals directly with special classes of private merchants, as in furnishing alcohol to wholesale druggists and manufacturing chemists. Liquors confiscated as contraband are reported to him and, if found "pure," are added to the stock of the dispensary. Private persons "having liquor which they wish to keep for their own use may throw

[1] *Act of* March 6, 1896; § 3.   [2] *Ibid.*, § 21.

the protection of the law around the same by furnishing an inventory of the quantity and kinds to the state commissioner and applying for certificates to affix thereto."[1]

The county boards of control are composed each of three persons, appointed for a term of two years and paid a limited *per diem* and mileage.[2] They are the local mouth-pieces of the central board, all their legislative acts being subject to the approval of the central board. They supervise the operations of the local dispensary and, with the approval of the central board, may establish, in their discretion, additional dispensaries, provided written remonstrance be not made by a majority of the voters of the township.[3] Local dispensers are appointed by the county board. The local dispenser must make oath "that he is not addicted to the use of intoxicating liquors as a beverage," and give bond for the observance of all rules, particularly that he "will not sell intoxicating liquors at a price other than that fixed by the state board of control."[4] In making sales he must require of purchasers formal written requests made on prescribed blanks furnished by the central board of control, consecutively numbered and to be strictly accounted for. Dispensers are required to remit weekly all moneys accruing, due the commonwealth, to the commonwealth treasurer, forwarding at the same time a duplicate statement to the central board of control. The law declares that appointments of dispensers "shall be deemed trusts reposed in the recipients thereof, not as matters of right but of confidence, and may be revoked upon sufficient showing by order of the county board of control."[5] Central control of dispensers, however, which is the crucial test of the efficacy of the system, is indirect, being reached by the control of the central board over the county boards. This fact has led to strong recommendations that the county

[1] *Act of* March 6, 1896; § 35. [2] *Ibid.,* § 9.
[3] *Ibid.,* § 7.   [4] *Ibid.,* § 8.   [5] *Ibid.*

boards be abolished, on the ground that they "do not control." [1]

The profits to the commonwealth arise from the wholesale trade with local dispensaries. The profits of the retail trade, after paying local dispensary expenses, are divided between the county and the municipality in which the dispensary is located.[2] As a matter of fact, the distinction between the wholesale and the retail trade is merely a device for convenience of book-keeping. The central board of control determines not only the wholesale price but the retail price; liquors in the hands of local dispensers are regarded as the property of the commonwealth, and losses arising from the defaults of local dispensers, or the destruction of the local stock, are charged against the central dispensary. Finally, local opposition may be punished by a withholding of all profits: "If the authorities of any town or city, in the judgment of the state board of control, do not enforce this law, the state board may withhold the part going to the said town or city, and use it to pay state constables or else turn it into the county treasury."[3]

(2) OPERATION

The volume of business done by the dispensary may fairly be judged from the following figures found in the report of the central board of control for the year 1897:

Liquors purchased by board of control............................ $780,503.42
Liquors sold to local dispensaries 1,125,674.35
Gross sales of local dispensaries 1,252,289.08
Net profits of local dispensaries................................ 84,782.78
Profits from beer and hotel dispensaries........................ 26,108.20
Average stock in central and county dispensaries............... 300,000.00

There were ninety local dispensaries in operation throughout the commonwealth in 1897. The profits to the commonwealth from the establishment of the business down to the close of the year 1897 may be approximated by a compilation of statements contained in official reports and the messages of the governor, as follows:

For 19 months ending Jan. 31, 1895	$110,348.80
For 11 months ending Dec. 31, 1895	133,467.77
For 12 months ending Dec. 31, 1896	200,000.00
For 12 months ending Dec. 31, 1897	146,443 09
Total (four years and six months)	$590,259.66

The reports of auditing committees of the legislature show that during the years 1895 and 1896 losses to the commonwealth on account of "balances due by ex-dispensers" amounted to $12,702.82.[1] These losses are attributed by the governor to "negligence on the part of the county boards of control," and are made an additional argument for the abolition of these boards.[2] The demoralization of the business by adverse decisions of the courts undoubtedly contributed to these results.

Although the management of the dispensary has been continuously in the hands of the party that instituted it, each succeeding administration has found much fault with the methods employed by its predecessor.[3] The difficulties which have interfered with its business success have arisen partly from the imperfections of an experimental organization, partly from the hostility of the courts to the theory of the system, and partly from the popular resistance to its rigorous restrictions upon privileges of trade. The organization has been gradually improved, first, by specializing the central management in a board of control apart from the

[1] See *Report of Board of Control*, 1898.   [2] *Message of* 1897.

[3] See, *e. g.*, *Message of Gov. Evans*, February 10, 1896, p. 6; *Message of Gov. Ellerbe, Session of 1898*, p. 4.

ordinary executive departments of the commonwealth; and, secondly, by concentrating responsibility in this board for the entire business management. To complete the potential efficiency of the organization, local dispensers must be brought under an effectual and direct central control. The central board makes but one recommendation in its report for 1897, which is as follows: "We find that the county boards of control are costing more than $10,000 per annum, and do not meet the requirements of the dispensaries, and recommend that they be abolished and some more suitable and economical plan be devised for local supervision and control." The proposal is evidence of the fitness of the central board, for the filling of a hundred offices is an element in the spoils of party victory which no practical politician can disregard. If current report may be credited, the board of control shows much business sagacity. A news item in the public press, under date of April 21, 1898, says: "The board of control in South Carolina, which has control of the state dispensaries of liquors, at its sitting on Monday ordered seven car-loads of beer, in order to avoid the prospective war-tax on that amount of supplies."

The validity of the political theory of the law has been severely tested. The fabric out of which institutions are made in South Carolina must be of a tough fibre, otherwise the dispensary system would long ago have been destroyed by judicial decisions. Active opposition on the part of the courts of the commonwealth was soon silenced by changes in their personnel. Adverse judgments of the federal courts continued to cause much trouble until a decision of the United States Supreme Court in May, 1898, set the law upon a fairly firm footing. The cases before the federal courts which involved the business administration of the law naturally arose under the interstate commerce provisions of the federal constitution.   In the two important cases which reached the United States Supreme Court, the essential question was as to the right of the commonwealth, under the permissive Act of Congress, [1] to control an import trade in liquors otherwise than by prohibition.   The decision in the earlier case, while it seemed to invalidate, in terms, only those provisions of the law which forbade free importation of liquors for private use, was susceptible of further application.   It declared that "when a state recognizes the manufacture, sale and use of intoxicating liquors as lawful, it cannot discriminate against the bringing of such articles in and importing them from other states." [2]   This dictum, taken together with the doctrine long maintained by the court that the right of commercial importation implies the right of subsequent sale, was afterward relied upon by the circuit court in upholding the right of importers to sell in "original packages." "This led," says the governor, "to the opening in the state of hundreds of private liquor-houses, and flooded the whole of South Carolina with whiskey." [3]   When this doctrine came up for review in Washington, a distinct administrative question was involved, namely, whether the commonwealth might, through its officers, decide what brands of liquors should fill the channels of trade in South Carolina.   In the later of the two cases it was held that such action is not to be regarded as discrimination against citizens of other commonwealths when the officers are allowed discretion to choose between home producers and outside producers. [4]   The objection— that administrative discretion as applied to purchase for exclusive sale by the commonwealth amounts to governmental discrimination against other commonwealths from

---

[1] *The " Wilson" Law of* August 8, 1890.

[2] Scott *v.* Donald, 165 *U. S.,* 58.   [3] *Message of* 1898.

[4] Vance *v.* Vandercook, 170 *U. S.,* 438.

which liquors are, in fact, not purchased,—was met by the court with the presumption that officers will buy fairly and in the open market, and with the assumption that, since private persons may import for their own use, the possible discrimination by officers of government is no more oppressive than the free discretion of private dealers.[1] The argument of the court upon this point hardly carries conviction. Doubtless the court would have held, as was held in the previous case, that an act of the legislature expressly discriminating in favor of home producers would be an unconstitutional infringement upon the trade interests of non-residents. From a commercial point of view it is difficult to see that the case is essentially altered by a change in the law giving to an executive board the power of discrimination which is forbidden to the legislature. As supporting a commercial doctrine, such an argument defeats itself by reason of its inclusiveness. It cannot stand except as based on police powers. The result of this decision, however, was to give assurance to the businesss management of the dispensary. Open sale by private persons having been definitely outlawed, the abuses of importation for " personal use " could more readily be reckoned with.

The monopoly features of the dispensary system array against it the hostility of the consumer, the merchant and the producer of liquors. The consumer resents restrictions upon his free choice of the place where he shall trade ; the dispensary, though its prices may be fair, is too huge to cater to the tastes of its customers as private interest compels private dealers to do ; and it is entirely wanting in social facilities. The would-be merchant is naturally antagonistic to a régime in which he finds his occupation gone ; but his position does not differ in theory from that of

[1] Vance v. Vandercook, 170 U. S,, p. 450-1.

would-be merchants in prohibition territory, whether the prohibition be local or general. It is upon the home producer that the dispensary as an economic institution bears with peculiar force. The dispensary sells at a monopoly price; but it buys at a price which is not only depressed by natural competition, but can be forced to the point of lowest living profit by governmental discrimination. Relying upon its police powers, the legislature gives to the board of control a general restrictive authority over manufacturers of liquors, to be exercised through the issue of licenses, and to be enforced by the drastic sanctions of summary seizure and confiscation of the product on hand.[1] When a merchant-commonwealth sets up with one hand a system of regulations upon production, with the other hand a monopoly of trade, and commits the administration of both to the wide discretion of a single board, the conditions seem favorable to economic oppression.

The retail trade in liquors, in general, illustrates in a high degree the law of increasing returns. It therefore offers a favorable field for commercial monopoly. This has been shown in the " tied house " system of Great Britain[2] and in the tendency of large liquor manufacturers in the United States to take the retail traffic into their own hands. Since the monopoly price of a commodity under the law of increasing returns tends downward and the volume of trade tends upward, the economic tendency of the dispensary as a legal monopoly is toward increased consumption of liquors. As an economic institution it is under economic law. The primary police purposes of the system, which favor diminution of consumption, run counter to this economic tendency.

---

[1] *Act of* March 6, 1896, § 15.

[2] *See Minutes of Evidence, Royal Commission* (*on the Liquor Licensing Laws*) *of April 15, 1896.*

It is characteristic, however, of all political schemes, that positive institutions tend to strengthen with time while negative precepts drop into disuse. The business management of the dispensary, in their struggle to establish the institution securely, have tended to relegate to the background the purely prohibitory ideal which inspired most of those who voted to establish the system, and have set up in its place a mercantile police ideal. Instead of establishing the dispensary that the traffic may be restrained, illicit traffic is repressed that the dispensary may flourish. The tendency of the dispensary is to push itself into territory previously under local prohibition and so to neutralize the operation of local option. Governor Tillman avowed it his policy to establish dispensaries wherever possible in order to crowd out the "blind tiger." At the legislative session of 1898, when a bill to exempt three prohibition counties from the operation of the dispensary law was before the house, it was alleged that, in one county, in the first year of the dispensary, liquor was bought to the value of $250; in the second, $5,000; and in the third, $10,000.

2. POLICE ADMINISTRATION

The powers of police control are practically centralized in the governor. They may be grouped in three classes: (1) discipline of local officers; (2) the constabulary and detective force; (3) the "metropolitan police" in cities. The law seeks to enlist the interested activity of sheriffs and magistrates in its enforcement by a grant of one-half the value of all liquors seized and confiscated through their efforts; but it provides, in addition to heavy penalties to which neglect of duty is liable through judicial proceedings, that these and other officers may be suspended by the governor.[1] The metropolitan police law, as enacted in 1894,

---

[1] *Act of* March 6, 1896, § 29.

authorized the governor, secretary of state and attorney-general, acting as a central board, to set up a board of police commissioners of their own appointment, in lieu of the local police authorities, in any municipality where the dispensary law was not enforced. The provision for appointment of constables and detectives has already been quoted.[1] The last two forms of centralization have rendered the first comparatively unimportant.

The constabulary are the aggressive agents of the dispensary for the protection of the commonwealth's monopoly. It is their province to examine all liquors shipped into the commonwealth, to seize liquors intended for unlawful traffic, to enter and inspect all places where liquors are kept, upon reasonable belief of unlawful intent, and, in case of seizure, to take steps for confiscation of the liquors and the punishment of the dealers.[2] Consequently the operations of the constabulary have given rise to the most dramatic incidents in dispensary history. The riots at Darlington and other places during the first year of the dispensary were precipitated by the exercise of the powers of search and seizure on the part of the constables.[3] Later it was found more efficacious to resort to the courts than to the shot-gun for protection against alleged violations of private rights. The work of the constables was sometimes pushed to an annoying extreme. A prominent resident of Charleston writes:[4] "Bishop C—— of the Protestant Episcopal Church told me himself of being accosted by a liquor constable who mistook the case containing the bishop's robes for a liquor drummer's case!" Governor Evans, commending the work of the constables, said: "If it were not for the espionage of these officers, the blind tiger would be rampant and the dis-

---

[1] *Act of* March 6, 1896, § 46; see Chapter III.

[2] *Act of* March 6, 1896, *passim.*   [3]See *The Liquor Problem*, p. 154 *ff.*

[4] *Letter of* Nov. 9, 1898.

pensary would not be self-sustaining." The activities of the constabulary became especially prominent in the conflict between the commonwealth administration and the federal circuit court. Liquors imported "for private use" having been seized by constables, an injunction was granted, in 1895, against interference, not only with the plaintiff in the case at bar, but with "any other person in the state of South Carolina as importer and consumer." Constables subsequently making seizures were committed for contempt. After the affirming of this decree by the Supreme Court in 1897,[1] Governor Ellerbe reported: "The state constables, under my instructions, seized quantities of whiskey where there were suspicious circumstances connected with its importation; but upon application to Judge S——, nearly all the whiskey seized was released."[2] Although the advanced position now assumed by the circuit court[3] removed "original package" agencies from the category of "blind tigers," it was still sought to suppress them as nuisances. A press dispatch from Charleston, dated a fortnight after the announcement of the circuit court's decision, gives this typical instance involving the action of the constabulary:[4]

Last week, J. S. P——, agent, opened an original package bar in Charleston and since then he has been reaping a harvest. To-day, however, a warrant was sworn out and the place was closed. . . . To-night the constabulary is in charge, taking stock and preparing to confiscate the whole outfit. The assistant attorney-general is here from Columbia to lead the legal fighting and the city is flooded with liquor constables.

The power of injunction again triumphed, for a time. Soon afterward the governor, recognizing that the court "had

---

[1] Scott *v.* Donald, 165 *U. S.*, 107. (Decree affirmed only as to "the parties named as plaintiff and defendants in the bill.")

[2] *Message of* 1898.   [3] Vandercook *v.* Vance, 80 *Fed. Rep.*, 786.

[4] *N. Y. Sun*, June 18, 1897.

practically paralyzed the constabulary," dismissed most of the force and left the responsibility for enforcement with the local authorities.[1]

During the years 1895 and 1896, the number of constables averaged 50. In 1896, the force numbered 55 and was divided and assigned to the "upper" and "lower" sections of the commonwealth, each division having at its head a chief constable. The cost of maintaining the force, being made by law a charge upon the dispensary fund, is reckoned as part of the expenses of operation. This cost was, in 1895, $43,032.01. As an offset the value of liquors confiscated or "contraband dumped" was set down at $17,031.70.[2] In 1897, when the efficiency of the force was most seriously impaired by adverse judicial decisions, leading to its partial disbandment, the cost of maintenance was $40,900.43; while the value of contraband seized amounted to only $4,634.52.[3]

The metropolitan police system has had extended trial in Charleston alone. The population of South Carolina in 1890 was 1,151,149; that of the metropolis was 54,995. In February, 1896, the number of South Carolina retail liquor dealers paying the special tax to the United States government was 387. This number included 88 dispensaries, leaving a total of 299 illicit dealers. Of the whole number of special-tax payers 167 were in the city of Charleston; this included 10 dispensaries, leaving 157 illicit dealers in the city.[4] Thus, while Charleston had less than five per cent. of the population of the commonwealth, and less than twelve per cent. of the dispensaries, it had more than fifty-two per cent. of the illicit dealers whose business was sufficiently assured to make it profitable to pay the internal revenue tax.

[1] *Message, Session of* 1898.   [2] *Message, Session of* 1897.
[3] *Report, Board of Control,* 1898.
[4] *Message of Gov. Evans,* February, 1896.

After the decision unfavorable to the law, in 1895, it was openly and flagrantly violated in Charleston. The mayor attempted to secure enforcement through the police, but the city council refused him support. The commonwealth's police commission, after repeated warnings to the city, took action, appointing a police board consisting of three "native born Charlestonians."[1] The report of this board showed a considerable decrease in arrests for drunkenness and disorder, and an increase in the proportion of successful prosecutions of illicit dealers, two members of the city council being among those indicted. Increase in dispensary receipts, which are the peculiar and unquestionable test of efficiency, as efficiency must be reckoned in South Carolina, was the conclusive proof of improvement, the annual profits being about doubled under the "metropolitan" police administration. The mayor of Charleston declined to state his judgment of the efficacy of the metropolitan system.[2] The governor under whom it was instituted in Charleston declared that it "has proved a success in every sense of the word."[3] Respecting the other cities of the commonwealth he reported in the same message: "The municipal authorities in every instance have shown a desire to co-operate with the state administration in enforcing this law." The milder discipline of withholding profits from a town has also been resorted to. In this procedure the central board of control acts, but the governor, as head of the constabulary, practically controls. For 1897 the governor reports: "So far the profits have been withheld only from the town of Sumter, and I have appointed a constable, to be paid out of the town's share of the profits, to see that the law is enforced there."[4]

Police administration is an ancillary element in the dis-

[1] *Message of* 1897, pp. 11–12.　　　　[2] *Letter of* Feb. 24, 1898.

[3] *Message of* 1897.　　　　　　　　　　[4] *Message of* 1898.

pensary system. It may properly be treated as a part of the commercial establishment in South Carolina, just as the system of special agents may be treated as a part of the excise revenue establishment in New York. Police administration, as we have seen, is the prime element in the enforcement of simple prohibition, the town-agency system being merely an auxiliary, although commercial in character, to promote the efficacy of prohibition; but it is impossible to discuss the South Carolina constabulary apart from the positive institution which it serves. The constables are the sappers and miners in the warfare waged by the dispensary against illicit competition. So soon as the ground has been won by the constabulary, the dispensary advances and intrenches itself with the security of a strongly capitalized commercial establishment. Prohibition means continual repression. The dispensary adds the efficacy of substitution. The dispensary interferes, we may say, merely with the manner of drinking, while prohibition seeks to exclude the fact. Forms may be changed by vigorous measures, which, though they meet with temporary resistance, are finally acquiesced in through force of circumstances. Appetites, on the other hand, refuse to yield to force until it becomes overpowering. The dispensary having been once firmly established in a community, public sentiment now generally sustains it to a sufficient extent to assure a reasonably efficient police administration by the local authorities.

The important exception to the rule is found in the case of large cities, where social and criminal impulses join in opposition to a system which makes the place where liquor may be obtained "the most dismal place in the town." Here the problem of repression reappears, and again it is difficult to conceive of a practical solution except by the process of substitution. Club life is characteristic of cities; even a "metropolitan" police cannot restrain the social instinct; and when it is associated with the strong desire for drink it would seem necessary to meet it on its own ground. The diversion of an appetite for intoxicating liquor to a liking for non-intoxicating drink will doubtless be more difficult than the substitution of the dispensary for the open saloon. It is a part of the liquor problem, however, and until it approaches solution repressive administration in cities will meet but qualified success.

3. SPREAD OF THE DISPENSARY IDEA

Until the monopoly plan was vindicated by the Supreme Court of the United States, South Carolina monopolized the theory of it more completely than she monopolized the traffic within her borders. Since that time this method of regulation has been urged, in various forms, in several other commonwealths. In most cases the central control given to the administration in these propositions has been slight. In such cases the dispensary idea ceases to be significant to this discussion. A peculiar system, which may induce central control for revenue, is that proposed for Alabama, in which municipal dispensaries, licensed by county authorities, are to be taxed by the commonwealth as private dealers have heretofore been taxed. Here, however, as in Georgia, the local dispensary system is not even a general system, but is instituted either by special legislation or by local option. A highly centralized dispensary scheme, which seems to better the example of South Carolina, is contemplated in the constitutional amendment adopted in November of 1898 by the people of South Dakota. The constitution under which this commonwealth entered the Union in 1889 prohibited the manufacture and sale of intoxicating liquors. This prohibition was repealed in 1896 by a popular vote of 31,901 as against 24,910. The majority for the dispensary proposition was only 1,613. It provides that

"The manufacture and sale of intoxicating liquors shall be under exclusive state control and shall be conducted by duly authorized agents of the state, who shall be paid by salary and not by commission. All liquors sold shall be first examined by a state chemist and the purity thereof established." The progress of the dispensary idea in the West will be watched with interest.

III. *Theory*

One of the reasons why the town-agency system is properly classed as archaic, despite instances of its continued existence, is that it does not appear in the modern, Western types of prohibition. The town agency comes into competition with an illicit but irrepressible private traffic. Commonwealth governments of the modern American type are unwilling to sacrifice their prerogatives and assume the responsibilities of private economic persons for such meager objects. The retail traffic must be either wholly private or wholly public. Hence the tendency of the day, observable in some quarters, to accept the fact that the liquor traffic cannot be suppressed and, where the regulation of private dealers cannot be made effectual, to exclude them entirely, leaving this field of trade free to the commonwealth. In Europe some governments enter into competition with private business; but even there the field usually comes to be occupied exclusively either by private enterprise or by the government. An interesting analogy is afforded in the field of railroad enterprise, in which competitive struggles between private lines and government lines are leading, as in Belgium, to the absorption of all lines by the state, and have already resulted, as in Germany, in a practical governmental monopoly of railroad transportation. In the United States the field of railroad management was, at an early day, abandoned, almost universally, to private enterprise; and to-day,

after extended experience with private competition and com-
binations, there is a very considerable public demand for
governmental ownership and management. The franchise
granted the railroad is analogous to the license granted the
liquor dealer. Both are granted on grounds of public convenience, and are subjected to peculiar regulations because
liable to great abuses. In so far as the liquor traffic is
regarded as a necessity, the argument for governmental management of it is based broadly on grounds of public welfare,
as is that for governmental management of railroads.

Governmental management and monopoly of the liquor
traffic is to be placed on very different grounds from ordinary trade monopolies of government. The tobacco monopoly of the French government, for example, is essentially a
revenue expedient. Moreover, being a mere control of the
product, for distribution to licensed dealers, the state administration does not extend to the consumer. The distinct
consideration of public health and morals which characterizes
a police measure is wanting in such revenue schemes. The
dispensary insists that the liquor traffic shall be safeguarded
at the danger point; it provides that an agent of government
shall execute its mandates in dealing with the individual; it
imposes on an officer who has no pecuniary interest in the volume of the traffic the responsibility of refusing to sell when
sale involves a menace to the safety of society; and, in the
centralized form, it seeks efficiency both in business management and in police restraints by the unification of a wide-
spread enterprise and an effective administrative control.

When the government enters the field of trade for purposes
of revenue it places itself on the level of the individual, and
its action must be affected, more or less, by the same motives
of self-interest that quicken individual enterprise. When, on
the other hand, its economic activities are undertaken primarily for the general welfare, government identifies its in-

terests with those of society and is moved by considerations of social uplift rather than by those of financial advantage. There is no economic warrant for governmental enterprise in a field already fully occupied by private enterprise. If it be a legitimate business, private self-interest will make it produce more than can be got out of it by the state; and the state will find it more profitable to secure its revenue by judicious taxation than by destroying the subjects of taxation by assuming a monopoly. The only justification, therefore, of the invasion of such a field by the state is the immediate advantage of society.

The socialization of the liquor traffic on the "Gothenburg plan" has precisely this object. In many respects the Norwegian "company" system bears a striking likeness to the American dispensary system.[1] It largely eliminates the motives of private gain, both from the management of the enterprise and from the work of dealing out liquor to the consumer; employés are salaried, and shareholders are paid only a prescribed rate on their investment. Since all profits go to the town treasury, to be distributed to objects of social advantage in which the management of the enterprise are interested, it may fairly be said that the government, representing society, is the beneficial entrepreneur. The shareholders individually are pecuniarily interested only in the stability of the scheme as a conservative investment; so far as there is any speculative interest, it is that of society. The police restrictions attached to the traffic by the company's by-laws, and in its contracts with the agents, are framed, of course, to suit the social conditions and usages of the country; but the approval of such regulations by royal sanction, and the general supervision of the administration of the system exercised by the governor of Gothenburg, lend the plan a *quasi*-governmental character that is suggestive also of the

[1] See *The Gothenburg System*, by E. R. L. Gould, Washington, 1893.

dispensary administration. If we assume that the Georgia city which establishes a local dispensary issues bonds to some of its leading citizens to provide current capital for the business, the financial interests involved would be precisely the same as in Gothenburg. The management of the system, however, instead of being in the hands of a selected group of the socially fit, is likely, in the American city, to be in the hands of an elected group of the politically available. The more aristocratic traditions and the more clearly defined class distinctions of society in Europe afford a natural social leadership, and make social action successful in fields which in the United States are given over to political action. Moreover, the moral status of the liquor traffic throughout Europe admits a participation in its management without loss of caste. In the United States the "better classes," even if it were possible, by concerted social action, to make the liquor traffic less harmful to the common people, are as yet unwilling to soil their hands with it. A permissive establishment of the company system for municipalities has been strongly urged in Massachusetts within this decade, and has even received a large vote in one or the other house of the legislature.[1] The plan has been urged with various political additions, such as the introduction of some judicial control, and a considerable degree of legislative prescription as to the distribution of profits, together with a larger share of municipal activity and a correspondingly narrower field of voluntary social action.[2] The voluntary-municipal plan of management gives slight promise of success. If it be a community affair it must be given official management, and local official management of so active an interest as the liquor traffic would mean, in most of our large cities, local official corruption.

[1] Such a bill passed the House by a vote of 132 to 39, May 15, 1894.

[2] See Dr. Gould's articles in *Atlantic Monthly*, Oct., 1893; *Forum*, Mar. 1894, etc.

The liquor traffic, like other branches of trade, is tending toward monopoly. The economic impulse tends to make it a commercial monopoly for the enrichment of the individuals who form the "combine." The social impulse would make it a social monopoly for the advantage of society; while the political impulse would make it a state monopoly for the peace and well-being of the state, which comprises society. The company system represents the socialization of the traffic; the dispensary system represents the state socialization of the traffic. State socialization in the form of the local dispensary depends for its efficacy as a means of social betterment upon local political authorities; and these authorities reflect the average standards of that portion of of the community which takes an active interest in politics. Where there is no betterment, the remedy is sought, in the American system, through political pressure. The Norwegian principle of social selection having been supplanted, in the control of the dispensary, by the principle of political representation, the remedy which might in the one case be found in a more active class coöperation must, in the other case, be afforded by territorial coöperation. And in order to bring the general standard to bear with greatest efficacy upon local conditions, as well as to insure coöperative efficiency in business administration, the entire administration throughout the body politic is unified and centralized under administrative control.

CHAPTER V

JUDICIAL ADMINISTRATION

BESIDES the various forms of direct administration and control, an indirect control may be exercised by the central administration through the courts. This form of control is indirect as applying to the subject-matter involved, namely, the liquor traffic, or, in case of neglect of duty, the delinquent officer; but it is direct as involving the immediate activity of the central administration in proceedings before the courts. By judicial administration, as the term is employed here, is meant, of course, not the administration of justice by the courts, but the activity of the executive department of justice. This activity may be shown either in the instituting and maintaining of judicial proceedings directly, or in the exercise of a power of control over local prosecuting officers. It may further include powers of prosecution vested in other departments of the executive branch of the government. The powers exercised may, in any of these forms, extend not only to criminal prosecutions for violations of liquor laws, but to preventive measures, such as petitions for injunction, and to civil actions, brought in the name of the officer instituting the proceedings, as for the recovery of the penalty on a bond. The practical administrative question presented by this division of the general subject is: To what extent, through what officers and by what processes can the central administration invoke judicial aid in the enforcement of the liquor policy of the commonwealth?

This field of our inquiry overlaps in part each of the other four, but, inasmuch as it has to do chiefly with the enforcement of penal sanctions, it is especially supplementary to the subject of repressive police administration. That subject, however, is involved in each of the other three forms of administration which we have considered. Every plan of regulation, whether based upon revenue or police, having laid down the law, calls for the vigilance of the police officer, and, in case of violation, the retribution of the courts. In order to facilitate the enforcement of restrictive liquor laws, provision is also made in some instances for special methods of procedure. The subject may thus be divided into three parts: (1) central control of local prosecuting officers; (2) special powers of central officers in judicial proceedings; and (3) special rules of procedure.

In some respects judicial administration lends itself more readily to centralization than any other branch of liquor law enforcement. The justice and the sheriff, in the early days of England after the conquest, were the representatives of the crown, and although these officers came later under local responsibility yet uniformity of procedure was secured by that complete system of centralized judicial authority which built up the English common law. Prosecuting officers could not escape the indirect control of a centralized judiciary, especially after the development of the office of public prosecutor. The enforcement of general criminal laws both physically, through the sheriff, and judicially, through prosecution, is traditionally, therefore, for the United States, a proper subject of central control.

I. CENTRAL CONTROL OF LOCAL PROSECUTING OFFICERS

Central control of local prosecutions is very common. It is generally conferred in the form of an alternative authority given to the central department of justice either to institute proceedings originally or to direct local prosecutors. An old

Missouri liquor law, for example, which confers license discretion upon the county court, provides that the attorney
general shall take special care to secure the collection of
fines.[1] The New Hampshire prohibitory law, while requiring the county solicitor to prosecute all violations, provides
also that the county solicitor shall act "under the direction
of the attorney general."[2] No power of discipline is given
the attorney general, however; the delinquent officer is
merely liable to heavy penalties on conviction of malfeasance or non-feasance. The fact that the legislature of 1895
increased the penalties prescribed for delinquent solicitors
and selectmen from a maximum of $200 to an absolute
penalty of $300, along with a general strengthening of leg-
islative safeguards, indicates the inefficacy of mere judicial
control. The general laws of Delaware for the regulation of
the liquor traffic provide for the prosecution of all offenders
by the attorney general, who may retain a commission of ten
per cent. on all collections; he may take out a bench warrant or a *capias* in the case of absconders, and put it in the
hands of any sheriff.[3]

The prohibitory laws in some of the western common-
monwealths have entailed an unusual development of centralized judicial administration. In North Dakota, in lieu of
police centralization, this sort of control is made peculiarly
strict. The prohibitory law provides that whenever, "for
any reason whatever, the provisions of this chapter shall not
be enforced in any county it shall be the duty of the attorney general to enforce the same in such county; and for
that purpose he may appoint as many assistants as he shall
see fit;" and the county then becomes liable to the attorney
general to the extent of $10 for each count upon which con-

[1] *Law of* Mar. 25, 1845.   [2] See *N. H. Laws*, 1878 and 1895.
[3] *Revised Statutes* (1893), Title VIII, ch. 531.

viction is secured.[1] Kansas provides similarly for prosecutions of violations of the prohibitory law in default of prosecution by the county attorney, and adds judicial penalties to the extent of forfeiture of office. The attorney general also has the authority, in common with county attorneys and citizens of the county generally, to petition for injunction upon illicit traffic.[2] Kansas has also provided for an action in the nature of a *quo warranto*, to be brought by the attorney general or his assistant for any county, against the mayor and councilmen of any city of the second class in which the prohibitory law is not enforced.[3] In the larger cities, as we have seen, the remedy is the appointment of a " metropolitan " police board.[4] In the present case, however, a successful action is simply followed by a judgment of ouster against mayor, councilmen and police force[5]—a fairly clean sweep of the city government.

A particularly radical and explicit provision for central action in judicial proceedings is found in the dispensary law of South Carolina, as follows:[5]

That when any solicitor neglects or refuses to perform any duty, or to take any steps required of him by any of the provisions of the preceding section, or by any of the provisions of this act, the attorney general, on his own motion, or by the request of the governor, shall in person, or by his assistant, proceed to the locality and perform such neglected duty, and take such steps as are necessary in the place of such solicitor, and at his discretion to cause a prosecution to be instituted, not only in the matter so neglected, but also a prosecution against the solicitor for malfeasance or misfeasance in office, or for official misconduct, or for other charges justified by facts, and to pursue the prosecution to the extent of a conviction and dismissal from office of any such solicitor. And in such event the attorney general shall be, and is hereby, authorized and empowered to appoint one or

---

[1] *Code* (1895).   [2] *Kansas General Statutes* (1889), § 2533.

[3] *Ibid.*, § 742; *Laws of* 1887, ch. 100.   [4] See Chapter III.

[5] *Act of* March 6, 1896, § 22.

more additional assistants, who shall each have while actually employed the same compensation, to be paid from the litigation fund of the attorney general. Any duty herein imposed upon a solicitor may be performed with equal force and effect by the attorney general or other person authorized by him to perform such duty.

The powers of original prosecution thus conferred upon the attorney general have been freely exercised. The governor and the attorney general have usually been in accord in their disposition to enforce the law; but the power given either to cause the instituting of proceedings independently of the other enhances the potential efficacy of the plan.

The authority of the governor, in some commonwealths, to control the conduct of the local prosecuting officers may be regarded, in a broad sense, as part of the controlling power of the central department of justice; the governor being nominally, though often not actually, the general head of the administration. This authority of the governor approaches very closely the power of police control proper, and is often associated with it. The association of the two is well illustrated in the administrative sanctions for the enforcement of prohibition in Maine. We have seen how ineffectual were the sanctions provided for the control of sheriffs and county attorneys by the law of 1872.[1] In 1880, the defect was remedied in form if not in effect, so far as judicial administration was concerned, by this provision:[2]

Whenever the governor shall, after investigation and hearing of the parties, be satisfied that any county attorney has wilfully neglected or refused to discharge the duties imposed upon him by this act, it shall be his duty to remove such attorney from office and fill his place by appointment.

The specific duties of the county attorney here referred to are to summon witnesses before the grand jury, to direct inquiries faithfully and to prosecute with vigor. Since the

---

[1] See Chapter III, p. 71.　　　[2] *Acts of* 1880, ch. 247, § 5.

governor is empowered to appoint constables for the immediate police enforcement of the law, central control of the circuit of penal administration seems here to be theoretically complete.

2. SPECIAL POWERS OF CENTRAL OFFICERS IN JUDICIAL PROCEEDINGS

The central activities just described arise directly from the police provisions of liquor laws; and the enforcement of police provisions naturally falls to the central department of justice. The other important aspect of liquor legislation, namely, revenue, may more properly involve the activity of a separate branch of the administration. Various powers are given the general revenue officers of the several commonwealths to safeguard the excise revenue by judicial proceedings. The most comprehensive powers are given to the department of excise in the commonwealth in which this branch of administration is most highly specialized, New York.

The prosecuting authority of the central department of excise in New York extends, first, to the discipline of local officers. The disciplinary power of the governor over local officers extends, as we have seen, to removal from office of delinquent county treasurers and district attorneys.[1] The judicial agencies of discipline that may be invoked by the commissioner of excise are much more comprehensive. Any officer failing to do any duty imposed by the excise law is liable to a penalty of $500, which the commissioner is specially empowered to sue for in his own name. The penalty, in case of recovery in such an action, accrues to the central treasury.[2]

The commissioner of excise may likewise maintain an action in his name as commissioner to recover the prescribed penalty for any violation of the law by an authorized dealer,

[1] See Chapter I, p. 29.   [2] *New York Liquor Tax Law*, (1898); § 42.

upon the bond of such dealer. Such an action may be commenced without any previous conviction for violation of the
law or for breach of the conditions of the bond.[1] A peculiar and supplementary authority is also given the commissioner to bring action in any such case for a specific penalty
of $50.[2] This penalty is cumulative and can be recovered
only by the commissioner, to the use of the commonwealth.
Actions of these two sorts have frequently been maintained.
In a typical case of an action brought on the ground of
illegal sales of liquor on Sunday, it was held that the liability of the surety for the full penalty on the bond may be
established upon proof of any violation of the law, and that
the liability of the principal for a fine or penalty is not a
condition precedent to the liability of the surety; thus sustaining the independent authority of the commissioner of
excise to bring his action. The usefulness of the provision
for actions of this sort is thus set forth by the commissioner
of excise :[3]

In some localities it appears that juries will not regard either law or
evidence in excise cases. In some instances they have carried their
contumacy so far as to be reproved or discharged by courts for being
controlled by unreasonable bias. Where this condition has prevailed
the department has resorted occasionally, with good results, to the
penalty provisions of section 42 of the law, or to such other civil proceedings as seemed advisable under the particular circumstances.

After conviction and sentence in any case of prosecution
of a dealer who has given bond, if the penalty imposed remains unpaid, the commissioner of excise is given exclusive
authority to bring action on the bond of the judgment debtor
to recover the penalty, without waiting for the issue of an
execution.[4]

In case a liquor tax certificate has been granted on false

[1] *Ibid.*, § 18.   [2] *Ibid.*, § 42.

[3] *Report*, 1899, p. 17.   [4] *N. Y. Liquor Tax Law* (1898); § 36.

representations, or in way contrary to law, " any citizen " may petition for an order of court revoking such certificate.[1] Such application may thus be made by the commissioner or any of his deputies, and it appears to be the proper recourse of an officer who has erred in issuing a certificate.[2] This process is the correlative of the *certiorari* proceedings, whereby the wrongful refusal of an officer to issue a certificate may be remedied.[3] In case of unlawful traffic under any conditions, any excise officer of the commonwealth, as well as any taxpayer of the county, may apply for injunction upon such traffic, and violation of such an injunction is punishable as contempt.[4]

The report of the commissioner for the first full year of the law's operation shows that the department instituted injunction proceedings in eleven cases, eight of which were successful.[5] In twenty-two cases proceedings were commenced by the department, and in fifty-three by private citizens, to revoke and cancel liquor tax certificates.[6] The full report to the legislature of 1899 has not yet been published. A recent case reported in the press illustrates the province of the commissioner. The petition of the commissioner had alleged that the defendant permitted liquors to be drunk on the premises under a liquor tax certificate authorizing the sale of liquors, no part of which was to be drunk on the premises; an order was granted revoking and cancelling the certificate.[7]

These powers of the central excise administration in New York, while in many respects penal, are based upon the financial scheme of the liquor tax law. At the same time they may be taken as illustrative of litigant powers enjoyed

---

[1] *Ibid.*, § 28, subdiv. 2.

[2] *Ibid.*, § 34, subdiv. 2.

[3] *Ibid.*, § 28, subdiv. 1.

[4] *Ibid.*, § 29.

[5] *Report*, 1898, p. 24.

[6] *Ibid.*

[7] *New York Evening Post*, Jan. 3, 1899.

by any separate branch of the central administration which is specially charged with the enforcement of the liquor laws. Thus the central liquor commissioner under the prohibitory régime in Massachusetts and in other commonwealths had special powers in instituting proceedings; as has also the central board of control of the South Carolina dispensary. These powers, however, when they apply to a mercantile system, tend to lose the character of prerogative and degenerate into the ordinary right of legal persons to maintain civil suits. A much more suggestive specialization of function is that contemplated in a recent proposition, which was rejected by the legislature of North Dakota, to provide a central "commissioner of temperance" to supervise the enforcement of the prohibitory law.

3. SPECIAL RULES OF PROCEDURE

The exigencies of penal administration of liquor laws have led legislatures into peculiar measures to secure the punishment of violations. Prohibitory laws have, naturally, been accompanied with particularly rigorous sanctions. Imprisonment has been made mandatory as part of the sentence; heavy fines have been prescribed; and the zeal of local officers has been encouraged, as against the restraints of prudence, by guaranty of indemnity in case of trespass upon private rights.[1] Thus the legislature holds out the deterrent or the inducement of personal interest to restrain evil doers and to encourage administrative activity. When centralized administration has been instituted, the problem is modified. Presuming upon the zeal of central officers, the legislature undertakes to facilitate their operations and obviate the obstructions that may arise in local judicial proceedings. The criminal quality of certain acts is specifically defined instead of being left to judicial determination; summary judicial proceedings are permitted in cases which ordinarily would

---

[1] See, *e. g., Mass.: Acts of* 1855, ch. 215.

call for jury trial; personal immunities are more or less abrogated, and the operation of provisional remedies is restricted. Such modifications of ordinary procedure are not peculiar either to liquor legislation or to centralized administrative systems; but some of the most notable illustrations of such provisions are found in these connections.

A plan of regulation in which private traffic in liquors is prohibited is, of course, most consistent with an extension of the right of search and a narrowing of the sphere of individual immunity. An extreme instance of this policy is presented in the prohibitory-socialistic system of South Carolina. It is made the duty of all officers of police administration, on information that any "suspicious package in possession of a common carrier contains alcoholic liquors or liquids, to detain the same for examination for the term of twenty-four hours, without any warrant or process whatever."[1] In order to make this authority effective, these officers "may enter any railroad car, or express car, or depot, or steamboat or other vessel, without warrant, and make search for such contraband liquors, and may examine the way bills and freight books of such common carrier."[2] Every hotel handling dispensary liquors must permit officers to enter "at any time, day or night, without a warrant," to search for contraband liquors.[3] Liquors "which are contraband" may be seized without warrant, while in transit or after arrival, no matter in whose possession they are found.[4] Liability to forfeiture extends even to the means employed in transportation of liquors when such transportation is by night; "regular passenger or freight steamers and railway cars" are exempted from seizure, but all other vehicles, animals and accessories so employed may be confiscated.[5]

These are preliminary provisions. The case having come

---

[1] *Act of* Mar. 6, 1896; § 29.   [2] *Ibid.,* § 33,
[3] *Ibid.,* § 21.   [4] *Ibid.,* § 25.   [5] *Ibid.,* § 38.

into court, the whole procedure is made burdensome to the defendant. Proceedings for the confiscation of liquors seized may be carried on as *in rem*.[1] Any person claiming such liquors as his lawful property, when they are appraised at $50 or over, must file his claim with the central board of control, together with an approved bond in the penal sum of $500, conditioned for the payment of all costs in case the goods in question shall be judicially condemned.[2] In all forfeiture proceedings for illicit transportation the burden of proof is upon the claimant of the liquors to show that they are not contraband.[3] Provisions thus stringent in narrowing the guaranties of justice, to the possible damage of innocent persons, are justified on the ground of the necessity of discouraging all persons from contending against a centrally administered institution.

The extreme rigor of any law is found in the denial of remedies for wrongs committed by officers under color of enforcing the law. Herein such a radical measure as the dispensary law shows its most striking characteristics. It expressly forbids the entertaining of any action for damages against an officer for injury to person or property resulting from the exercise of the wide discretion conferred by the law,[4] and abrogates the usual provisional remedies.[5] It provides that liquors and vessels seized shall be irrepleviable.[6] This denial of the right of replevin in South Carolina irresistibly suggests incidents connected with " nullification " in 1832–3. The commonwealth, in her efforts to tame the rebellious impulses of some of her minor political units, has executed the teachings of the national government,—and she seems even to have bettered the example.

Definitive legislation declaring places where liquors are kept unlawfully to be nuisances is not uncommon in connec-

---

[1] *Ibid.*, § 27.   [2] *Ibid.*, § 31.   [3] *Ibid.*, §.39.
[4] *Ibid.*, § 22.   [5] *Ibid.*, § 45.   [6] *Ibid.*, § 22.

tion with a license system; but such provisions of law have attained their chief significance under prohibition and the dispensary system.   Kansas affords the most drastic illustrations of such provisions as well as the most instructive judicial interpretations thereof.   All places falling within the prohibitions of the Kansas law "are hereby declared to be common nuisances; and upon the judgment of any court having jurisdiction finding such place to be a nuisance under this section," it is to be abated by the proper officer "by taking possession thereof and destroying all intoxicating liquors found therein, together with all signs, screens, bars, bottles, glasses, and other property used in keeping and maintaining said nuisance."[1]   (Kansas having no official use for such liquors and appliances, the decree here is destruction, instead of confiscation as in South Carolina.)   The highly prescriptive character of the provisions quoted was well pointed out from both bench and bar in a case before the United States Supreme Court. Justice Field remarked: "The court is not to determine whether the place is a common nuisance in fact, but is to find it to be so if it comes within the definition of the statute, and, having thus found it, the executive officers of the court are to be directed to shut up and abate the place by taking possession of it."[2]   In arguing against the constitutionality of the act, counsel referred to it as giving jurisdiction to "a court of equity which is to act not as a court of justice but simply as a legislative agent, to register the decrees of a legislative body."[3]   The court, in its opinion, answered these objections, by confession and avoidance, thus:

The fact to be ascertained was, not whether a place kept and maintained for purposes forbidden by the statute was, *per se*, a nuisance—

---

[1] *Act of* Mar. 7, 1885; § 13.   Likewise in Iowa, *et al.*

[2] Kansas *v.* Ziebold, 123 *U. S.*, 623: Dissenting opinion.

[3] *Ibid.,—Brief of* Joseph H. Choate.

that fact being conclusively determined by the statute itself—but whether the place in question was so kept and maintained. If the proof upon that point is not full or sufficient, the court can refuse an injunction or postpone action until the State first obtains the verdict of a jury in her favor.[1]

Such rigid methods of determining the unlawful character of a specific act are less radical than some of the means provided for preventing and punishing the act. In an action to abate and enjoin the liquor nuisance, "the injunction shall be granted at the commencement of the action, and no bond shall be required." The fact of the nuisance, as defined by the law, having been shown to the satisfaction of the court, the injunction is made perpetual. "Any person violating the terms of any injunction granted in such proceeding shall be punished as for contempt."[2] Jurisdiction is thus given a court of equity over criminal acts punishable, under other sections of the same law, by indictment and jury trial. This virtual provision for enjoining crime has been vigorously assailed as contrary to the principles of the common law. "Government by injunction," whereby alleged criminal acts might be punished summarily as contempts, was assailed in the early liquor cases under the Kansas law, as in more recent cases in other fields, on the ground that such procedure involved a denial of the due process of law guaranteed by the Federal constitution. In the Kansas cases the Supreme Court held, however, that this was "a salutary jurisdiction" and that, "Though not frequently exercised, the power undoubtedly exists in courts of equity thus to protect the public against injury."[3] This view was more explicitly stated in the remarks of the court upon contempt punishments in an Iowa liquor case at a later date, as follows:

---

[1] *Ibid., Opinion, per* Harlan, J.

[2] *Act of* Mar. 7, 1885, § 13; *Kansas General Statutes* (1889), § 2533.

[3] Kansas *v.* Ziebold, 123 *U. S.*, 623.

"Certainly it seems to us quite as wise to use the processes of the law and the powers of the court to prevent the evil as to punish the offence as a crime after it has been committed."[1] The wide development of this doctrine has resulted in a reaction against it. The commonwealth which seems first to have brought it to public notice, being under the political control of a party whose national platform condemned the principle of "government by injunction," has undertaken to meet the difficulty by providing for two classes of contempts, one of which may be determined by the court, the other by a jury.[2]

The changing of established rules of judicial procedure, in order to secure particular ends, is always a menace to civil liberty, and generally fails to effect permanent improvement in the enforcement of law. In some instances, where a superior authority intervenes, the procedure relied upon to secure enforcement is employed against enforcement. It is a remarkable instance of retributive justice that the South Carolina dispensary law, which provided for the restraint of illicit traffic by an injunction procedure no less complete than that of Kansas, was practically nullified by injunctions issued from the Federal courts against the officers of the commonwealth. The dispensary law brought upon itself the intervention of the Federal Courts largely on account of its extreme invasion of the ordinary immunities of individuals. "If you examine the original act," writes a South Carolina professor, "you will find that Magna Charta, *habeas corpus* and provisions against searches and seizures are all disregarded."[3] Although these features are still prominent in the letter of the law, use has restricted their application in practice. The proper administrative organs are more generally relied upon for enforcement.

[1] Eilenbecker *v.* Plymouth Co., 134 *U. S.*, 31; *Opinion per* Miller, J.

[2] *Kansas, Acts of* 1897, ch. 106.

[3] *Letter of* Oct. 22, 1898.

"Courts of equity," says a recent writer, "can in no event be made to replace permanently an able and honest administration of its duties by the executive department of the government."[1] In Kansas the abnormal extension of judicial powers, for the uprooting of the prohibited liquor traffic, partly took the place of a centralized constabulary. Any citizen might apply for an injunction; individualization of judicial administration was set up. The same plan had been tried in other cases. Massachusetts attempted in the same way to insure the enforcement of prohibition in 1855.[2] The plan failed, and a centralized constabulary was provided, which, if it also failed ultimately to enforce the prohibitory law, at least made known to the people of the whole commonwealth that there was such a law on the statute-books. Summary powers of central control in the hands of the executive can hardly have a worse result than failure. Distorted extensions of the powers of the courts threaten the stability of our judicial system by involving it again in functions of ministerial administration from which political evolution has tended to set it free.

[1] W. H. Dunbar: *Government by Injunction* (*Publications of the American Economic Ass'n*), p. 43.

[2] *Act cited, ante.*

CONCLUSION

To one who considers the history of liquor legislation in the United States during the last fifty years, the decade now closing presents some features of peculiar interest. In some respects it has been a period of quiescence; at least one does not find so great a volume of liquor legislation as in some preceding periods, relatively to the general expansion of the statute-books. There has been a tendency in some quarters to gather fragmentary regulative measures, which had accumulated with years, into a coherent system. General provisions were, in some cases, especially in the south, substituted for a multitude of special local provisions. New centralized systems of administration were instituted in some commonwealths, as if to make sharp test of the practicability of long-tried but ineffectual plans of regulation. An inclination has been shown to look at the liquor problem rationally, from the legislative view-point, and to fix the legal status of the traffic in accordance with current social conditions, even if to do so should require a restatement of the problem. Certain broad lines of policy have been marked out in liquor legislation, which commend themselves to the student of political science as a rational basis of future action. Some of these lines of policy, or principles of action, have been limited in their application to one or a few commonwealths and may be difficult of application in others. Some may be regarded as radical or too liberal in that they relegate to the limbo of an obsolete past, or of a distant and doubtful future,

144   [482

theories which have been widely regarded as right and practicable. They are, however, part of the social and political development of the day. In so far as they comport with changes generally manifest in the organization and activities of society they may be regarded as natural; and in so far as they are productive of satisfactory results they must be accepted as pointing the path of progress.

Regulative plans and administrative forms are so intimately related that in any broad view of the political relations of the liquor traffic they must be considered together. The phases of current development which seem to merit special note are (1) The substitution of the liquor tax system for the license system; (2) The extension and elaboration of local option; (3) The contingent central control of city police administration; (4) Governmental management of the liquor traffic; and (5) The recognition of the general province of administration. These aspects of current legislation represent, in general, the conclusions which may be drawn from our study of centralized systems of administration. The first emphasizes the efficacy of natural and economic laws as an aid to governmental regulation of the liquor traffic; the second illustrates the force of communal sentiment in securing efficient administration; the third recognizes the final responsibility of the commonwealth administration for the maintenance of local order; the fourth carries this responsibility into the domain of actual traffic; and the fifth embodies some general conclusions as to the ideals to be kept in view in administrative organization.

Our study has shown that these developments accord, in general, with the laws of evolution. Local option represents natural, spontaneous differentiation among communities in imposing restrictions upon the right to sell. Governmental management of the liquor traffic affords peculiar opportunity for differentiation among individuals in the right to buy. Taxation, as a general regulator, represents a tendency to equilibration as opposed to an excessive development of such a policy of personal discrimination as is involved in a license system. Central administrative control of police is based upon a demand for a reasonable coherence in the activity of regulative agents throughout the body politic. Centralized administration in financial and commercial systems illustrates a trend toward a larger integration of administrative activity. At the same time, administrative efficiency has been seen to depend largely upon specialization of function.

I. TAXATION VS. LICENSE

One of the most approved means of restraining the evils of the liquor traffic heretofore has been discrimination among persons in the privilege of trade. One of the most notable traits of society to-day, however, is the growing disregard of personality. Character is merged into capability. This submergence of personality has become marked in liquor license administration. A crude manifestation of this condition is seen in the fact that many of the men who hold themselves out as retail dealers are merely agents of the great brewers. To pass upon the personal fitness of such an applicant for license is merely to interfere with a principal in the choice of his agent. But the same liberal doctrine of commercial freedom, which permits such consolidations, unites with the current democratic theory of personal equality in opposition to the whole policy of discrimination among persons in privileges of trade. The result is that even where the fitness of the applicant is to be judged *in propria persona*, the exercise of administrative discretion for purposes of restriction has become increasingly difficult. It is not merely that well-laid trains of corrupt influence vitiate, in many instances, the exercise of the discriminative power; the system tends to break down of its own weight by reason of the impracticability, under present conditions, of making fair discrimination. The business of the average saloon-keeper is one of the most sordid sorts of commercialism that claim the countenance of the state. To weigh the relative fitness of applicants who press for this privilege and to maintain against them all with even hand the interests of society requires the judicial temper of a Solomon and more than his moral stamina.

The tendency to substitute other checks, to a greater or less extent, for the discretion of license boards, is seen in the wide-spread policy of " high license." Although this policy is usually justified on the ground that the traffic should share the expense of protecting society against the evils which it foments, the high license " fee " is in reality a tax which, like a protective tariff duty, operates as a partial regulation of trade. To the extent to which it does so operate, the imposition of the tax is a police measure for the restraint of the traffic; and to the same extent it displaces the discretionary exercise of the power of restriction by administrative officers. To obviate entirely the evils of mal-administration of license, the legislature may prescribe definitely the conditions on which the traffic may be entered upon, one of the conditions being the payment of a regulative tax.

The prescribing of conditions precedent to engaging in the traffic retains all the restraints of license except personal discrimination; and the exaction of a heavy tax adds an automatic restraint. It recognizes the virtue of economic law and throws back upon such law the limiting of the number of drinking places. The tax in New York city, in the Boroughs of Manhattan and the Bronx, being $800, there was, in 1897-8, one saloon to every 280 of population. In Boston the license law limits the number of licenses to one to every 500 of population. If this number is sufficient (and there seem to be drinking places enough in Boston to supply all demands) then the New York tax might be considerably increased without impairing seriously the opportunities for drinking; and yet there has already been a considerable reduction in the number of saloons in New York since the enactment of the Liquor Tax Law. The raising of the tax to the point of desired limitation would, of course, raise the premium on evasions of the tax; but it would also make more valuable the franchise, so to speak, of lawful dealers. Competition for trade impels the dealer, whether licensed or taxed, to extend and hold his patronage; and it becomes his interest in increasing degree, as his franchise becomes more costly and more exclusive, to secure the suppression of the competing illicit and untaxed traffic. The liquor tax law gives some play to those indirect influences for law-enforcement which Professor Lester F. Ward attributes to what he calls "attractive legislation."[1] The tendency of this policy is thus to confine the "blind tiger" to remote and unattractive places, and to restrict its ravages. At the same time, by reducing the number of legalized saloons, it renders them less obtrusive and more capable of efficient police supervision.

The ministerial character of a simple revenue administration keeps the primary administration of the liquor tax law out of local politics. The tax collector is no respecter of persons. Such an administration also lends itself most readily to centralization, with its direct and indirect results for the improvement of administrative efficiency. If there be raised the question of the personal fitness of those who enter an open traffic, the testimony of the New York Commissioner of Excise may be adduced; his department " has found, by experience and investigation, that it is about the same identical people who follow the trade under this as under former

---

[1] *Dynamic Sociology*, I, 44.

laws."[1]   If there be any difference in the moral relation of the government to the traffic under license laws and under liquor tax laws, license implies an official approval whereby the government becomes, in a sense, sponsor for the con duct of the liquor dealer.   Under a taxing system, on the other hand, the position of the commonwealth government, toward a town which votes local prohibition, is more nearly analogous to that of the United States government toward a prohibition commonwealth.   In the decision in the License Tax Cases, which arose out of the collection of United States internal revenue taxes from liquor dealers when the traffic was prohibited in Massachusetts, Chief Justice Chase said: " There is nothing hostile or contradictory, therefore, in the acts of Congress to the legislation of the State.   What the latter prohibits, the former, if the business is found existing notwithstanding the prohibition, discourages by taxation. The two lines of legislation proceed in the same direction and tend to the same result."[2]

The special administrative restrictions with which the liquor traffic has been hemmed in have given it an artificial prominence in politics which has been productive of serious disadvantages.   As was formerly the case with the levee system along the muddy Mississippi, the bed of the stream rises almost as rapidly as its artifical boundaries.   It should be made, so far as possible, to scour its own channel.   The saloon, as an incident of social life, must, of course, have such police attention as its conditions demand.   So must a horse show or a charity fair.   But to whatever extent the traffic is legally permitted it should be placed upon a natural basis, and, so far as practicable, committed to the control of economic law.   Its malign interest in local politics may thus be diminished, and questions of regulation may be considered on their merits as matters of general policy.

[1] *Report,* 1899.   [2] 5 *Wall.,* 462, 473.

The withdrawal of license discretion from administrative officers must be conceded to be a departure from the general rule of administrative development. It is the recognition of a higher rule—that of social development. Society demands a certain amount of administrative coercion, in some spheres an increasing amount; but when the supply, in a particular sphere, becomes too great, or is of such a kind as not to yield the satisfaction sought, the demand falls off or is diverted to substitutes. No sooner had the policy of giving discretion to a more or less specialized license administration become generally developed than legislatures began to find it necessary to put closer and closer limits upon its exercise. First came limitations by statute, either general or special; then local option; then the substitution of taxation for license and the enlargement of the sphere of repressive police administration; lastly, the necessity of imposing restrictions upon legalized traffickers has been obviated entirely through the assumption of the traffic by the government. Society seems disposed to distribute its demand for preliminary restrictions upon the traffic among all these substitutes, regarding license discretion in this field as a relic of monarchy, most liable to abuse and unsuited to present conditions. License administration is thus tending to resolve itself into its two natural components, prescriptive legislation and penal administration. The dictum of the New York Court of Appeals, already cited, to the effect that "the imposition of conditions precedent is the distinguishing feature of a license law,"[1] merely recognizes that the legislative prescripts may exclude administrative discretion. When general restrictions wisely imposed by the legislature, respecting character and location, are supplemented with local option, whereby these restrictions may be made more definite, all the official discretion that is needed may be left to the penal administra-

[1] See Chapter III.

tion, to be exercised by that branch of government which is peculiarly qualified to exercise it, the judicial authority.

2. ELABORATION OF THE LOCAL OPTION POLICY

Another important change which has been progressing since the earlier prohibition era is in the direction of recognizing that the moral status of any business or practice is largely determined by the community immediately affected, irrespective of general legislation. Out of the moral consensus of a community comes the real power that gives efficiency to local administration. Despite the general bonds of nationality which unify the people of this country, the moral standards of different communities differ widely on some subjects, pre-eminently on the subject of the liquor traffic. The general tendency toward liberalism in matters of personal conduct has undoubtedly made for a lower average ideal of liquor restriction than prevailed fifty years ago. The infusion of foreign elements into our social aggregate has continually brought new ideals into competition with those older ones which in certain sections of the country might have reached a condition of general accord if left alone. As a result of these conditions, such a moral view of the liquor traffic as would lead to its prohibition does not prevail effectually throughout any single commonwealth; and the legislative sequence has been an extensive development of the plan of local option. The legislature having fixed the general standard of restriction at the average, local communities are left a measure of freedom to raise the standard to the highest point at which local sentiment will sustain its enforcement.

It is worth noting that the policy of special legislation, which has played so large a part in the regulation of the traffic in the south, is often merely local option in a form modified by environment. It was not merely that the town was the traditional unit of political action in the northern commonwealths while the south inclined to larger units; the extraordinary development of the policy of special legisla- tion in the south within the last quarter-century is rather due to the determination of the political aristocracy, especi- ally in the "black belt," to keep the government in their own hands.   The "ruling classes" in local communities could get what they wanted much more effectually through an act of the legislature than through a local plebiscite.   The ex- tension of actual local option in the south, with the corres- ponding decrease in special liquor legislation, in more recent years, has doubtless been promoted by the imposing of new restrictions upon the suffrage.

It is evident that local option affords an alternative means of escape from the abuses of license discretion.   The pre- scribing of conditions precedent definitely by the legislature opens the traffic to all; local prohibition closes it to all; and any degree of restriction imposed through local option, as through legislative action, operates uniformly as respects persons.   One of the most suggestive schemes of liquor regulation, and most rational in its promise of efficiency, is the combination of a centrally administered liquor tax sys- tem for the commonwealth generally, with a graduated plan of local option as to police restrictions.   Such a scheme has been well worked out in New York.

The New York provisions for local option allow the towns an unusually wide range of choice in respect to the degree of restriction; they thus facilitate the accurate registry of the local consensus on this subject and thereby contribute to the maintenance of administrative efficiency.   Just as com- monwealth prohibition was replaced by local option in order to secure territorial definiteness in the expression of popular sentiment, so the simple alternative of "saloon or prohibi- tion," which was formerly, and in some sections is still, presented to local option, has given place here to a wide choice as to the mode in which the traffic may be carried on.   When local sentiment favors "blue laws," the sale of liquor can be absolutely interdicted; and it is interesting to note that this was the stern decree of 263 of the 942 towns of New York in 1897–98.[1] The successively lower ideals of restriction may be expressed in permitting sales by pharmacists only; sales of liquor not to be consumed on the premises; sales by hotel-keepers to guests; or, finally, bar-room sales.[2] This plan permits the outlawing of the saloon, and, at the same time, the reserving of the individual right to buy and drink; it may thus secure that exclusion of the social element in the liquor traffic which is one of the chief claims of the dispensary system upon public favor.   The open saloon, with its seductive attractions, is the chief objective factor in the American liquor problem.   If it can be displaced the problem will be simplified.

Local prohibition frequently proves unsatisfactory; but it affords a means of restriction which is capable of development.   The exercise of option as to the manner of sale, by small and comparatively homogeneous communities, is most conducive to local police efficiency.   When, further, the complications which arise from the exercise of license discretion are excluded by a simple liquor tax system, and especially when the revenue administration is under effective central control, most of the conditions of law-enforcement are fulfilled.   If the general abolition of the liquor traffic is a social desideratum, it can be attained only by gradual advance, through the building up of public opinion by moral education and the conserving of the results thus gained by rational political means.   If "the saloon must go," its

[1] *Report of State Commissioner of Excise*, 1899.

[2] *Liquor Tax Law*, § 16.

departure will be made more speedy and permanent by permitting a reasonable measure of social choice in the use of less harmful agencies.

3. CONTINGENT ADMINISTRATIVE CONTROL OF CITY POLICE

Local option is admissible only when local ideals are higher than those fixed by the consensus of the commonwealth. To permit local option upon the question of abrogating generally recognized requirements of morality and order would be to sacrifice civilization to anarchy. The very notion of a general consensus, however, involving as it does an average of some sort, implies that some communities will fall below the standard, with the result that the local consensus cannot be relied upon to secure the enforcement even of the minimum restrictions. This is specifically the problem of the large city.

The problem may be somewhat restricted by the introduction of neighborhood option within the city. This is the principle actually practised in the requirement of " consents " of near-by residents or property-owners as a condition precedent to the establishment of a saloon. Ward option, election-precinct option and other similar plans are also applied to secure the exclusion of the legalized saloon from certain urban areas. But the city is one, and the very congestion which creates the social "down-draught" of the great city renders its population, as a whole, liable to the pernicious influences which prevail in the less favored quarters. Some conclusions may be framed upon the basis of past experiments and present conditions, as to the best way in which central control may be exercised to effect permanent improvement in the local enforcement of police regulations affecting the liquor traffic in cities.

The complete subversion of municipal independence in police administration has usually produced only temporary improvement. So soon as the various interests involved become adjusted to the new location of responsibility, the influences brought to bear upon the central executive and upon the officials whom he controls tend to lower the tone of centralized administration to that of local administration; sometimes, indeed, when the motive of the change is partisan advantage, the resulting administration has been worse than that which it displaced. At best, the maintenance of higher standards under centralized responsibility depends largely upon the determined and active moral sentiment of the wider constituency to which the governor is responsible; and, this granted, the invasion of a traditional sphere of local self-administration tends to alienate local sympathy and prevent the coöperation even of law-abiding people. Permanently centralized administration of city police has in rare instances accomplished notably good results. In the very nature of things, however, it must be regarded as a make-shift. Aside from its failure to develop the capacity of self-help in the city, and its various inherent weaknesses, permanent centralization is, paradoxical though the statement be, necessarily temporary. The vote of a single city is already, in one case, half the entire vote of the commonwealth. The vote of two or three large cities will soon control the government in several commonwealths. The forms of control should be shaped so as to train the great cities, so far as the influence of administration can be made educative, to self-control.

The rational course in this matter is, as in other parts of the liquor problem, the moderate course. A contingent, potential, administrative control, extending merely to the removal of police commissioners by the central executive, in his discretion, after hearing and for cause, combines most of the theoretical elements of efficacy. Various plans approaching this sort of control have been put forth by commonwealth legislatures. The care taken to avoid the possibility of an autocratic exercise of power by the governor has usually rendered these provisions nugatory. The power to appoint temporary special officers, to discharge duties neglected by local authorities, usually proves ultimately ineffectual because, even if they succeed for a time, when the duties of these officers terminate the old conditions reassert themselves with new force. The comparative failure of contingent plans of control heretofore should not be regarded as conclusive. In most cases of this sort, either the powers granted to the governor did not enable him to reach summarily the root of the difficulty, or general sentiment did not approve the plan of regulation which local authorities failed to enforce. By granting the traffic a natural status the way is opened for a healthy manifestation of the common sense as to the enforcement of necessary regulations; and by the efficient centralization of revenue administration, public opinion in the commonwealth as a whole is brought to bear more readily upon deficiencies of local police administration.

The preservation of the peace and the apprehension of law-breakers being a vital concern of the commonwealth, it cannot be given over absolutely to the chance control of local will. On the other hand, democratic institutions require for their preservation a large measure of local self-government and local administrative responsibility. Interference in local administration by the central executive should be regarded as an emergency power, like that of declaring martial law, to be exercised with vigor and directness when occasion requires, and to be laid aside as promptly. This policy will give confidence to good citizens, discourage lawlessness, compel conformity on the part of city administration to general standards and promote the welfare and moral concord of the commonwealth.

4. GOVERNMENTAL MANAGEMENT OF THE LIQUOR TRAFFIC.

The socialistic experiment into which South Carolina stumbled, when searching for a way of escape from threatened prohibition, cannot be regarded as an accident. It is quite in keeping with certain marked tendencies of current social thought. It embodies the idea of sumptuary freedom subject to merely formal restraints; and it illustrates the widening of the field of governmental activity. The elimination of the social feature in the liquor traffic is not peculiar to the dispensary system; and in the mere matter of excluding private enterprise the dispensary is only applying the familiar principle which underlies all prohibitory laws. Indeed, the cardinal element of the system, the assumption of the liquor traffic by the government, if considered as a business enterprise, is chiefly interesting as an illustration of socialistic theory.

The most significant contribution, perhaps, which the dispensary plan makes to current thought on the liquor problem is its unique and emphatic approval of the use of liquors as a beverage. Its disapproval of their abuse is, in theory, almost equally marked. The commonwealth, having undertaken to carry on the liquor business, is in position to exemplify most completely its ideal of the manner in which such a business should be carried on. Its rules for the conduct of the business are addressed to its own paid agents, and to this extent the framing of regulations is unhampered by the usual considerations of difficulties of enforcement. Since the dispensary system is held forth as being primarily a system of police regulation, for the general welfare, the lines of distinction which it draws between the use and the abuse of intoxicating beverages may be regarded as setting a convenient standard.

The lines of distinction among vendees, prescribed by the commonwealth of South Carolina for the regulation of its own traffic, do not differ materially from those prescribed in other commonwealths for the regulation of private traffic. Sales to certain defective and dependent classes are interdicted. Persons who are competent may buy without limit. The law assumes, until by their conduct they show the contrary, that these persons may safely be left to regulate their own appetites.

The distinction is a simple one; and yet all prohibitory laws disregard it. It is seldom urged in support of such laws that the use of liquors is *malum in se ;* but since men cannot be trusted to exercise moderation, all sales of liquor should be made *mala prohibita.* However good the grounds may be for such a contention, there is so strong a sentiment to the contrary in present-day society that it is important to differentiate the elements of the controversy. This might be done by distinguishing clearly those classes of persons who may be conclusively presumed incompetent to exercise self-control, and framing for men generally such reasonable regulations as they will abide by. So soon as an individual puts himself, by his conduct, into the non-competent class, peculiar restrictions should attach to him and to those who have dealings with him.

In earlier times in New England, when government was 'more keen to control the conduct of individuals and less ready to enter the fields of trade, selectmen were required to post lists of common drunkards, tipplers and gamesters in every place of sale; to furnish dealers in liquors with the names of idlers and excessive drinkers; and expressly to forbid sales of liquors to " any of the afore-described misspenders of time and estate." [1] The difficulty of enforcing even such specific discriminations is indicated by repeated acts for the strengthening of these restrictions and the increase of the penalties for their violation.[2] At the same

---

[1] *Mass. : Act of* Feb. 28, 1787.   [2] *Ibid.,* Feb. 12, 1819.

time, and throughout the colonial period, the recognition of the liquor traffic as necessary to the accommodation of the public is emphasized not only by the usual license laws, but by numerous laws prescribing a maximum price for liquors.[1] The progress of the principles of personal liberty and economic freedom has left such methods behind; but we have already come back, in the cycle of political development, to a higher degree of regulation of the liquor traffic—the assumption of trade by the government. The question now presented is, whether government should not also lay its hand, more effectually than in the period of the " blue laws," upon individual conduct—whether society, for the safeguarding of its own normal progress, should not exclude its abnormal members from consideration in framing general social regulations, by placing such abnormal members under peculiar legal tutelage. Such discrimination among persons may be difficult to carry into effect; but the finding of differences where they exist and the suiting of the treatment to the case is one of the ways of making things better, both in the physical world and in the body politic.

5. THE GENERAL PROVINCE OF ADMINISTRATION

If it be permitted to venture general characterizations of current history, it may be said that our commonwealths have generally entered upon a period of administrative development, as distinguished from the long preceding period of legislative expansion which, in turn, followed the revolutionary period of constitution-making. One of the most important indications of the progress of governmental ideas is the evolution of the administrative organization. Out of the diffusion of responsibility that marked early town administration has grown the imperial concentration of authority

---

[1] *E. g., So. Car., Statutes of* 1695; *Pa., Laws of* 1718, ch. 235 (1 *Sm. L.* 104); *Ga., Laws of* 1791.

which is found in the mayor of a modern city. From compulsory and non-professional service required of private citizens we have advanced to the maintaining of a professional class of public servants, limited, in some branches, to experts. Finally, for the unification of administration in matters of general concern, resort has been had to a wide variety of centralized commissions.

The increased regularity and definiteness resulting from more complete organization has necessarily reacted upon legislation. It has been said that "Government always administers more wisely than it legislates. . . . It is from the administrative, or executive, branch that has thus far come what little progressive action governments have ever taken."[1] Whether this be true or not, it is undoubtedly the tendency of administrative activity to clarify the purposes of legislative regulation, and to render the more effective service in this respect in proportion as expert ability is employed in administrative duties. In so far as administrative organization is made more nearly perfect for the enforcement of liquor laws, the improvement of those laws will be promoted. It may also be true that " Every extension of the regulative policy involves an addition to the regulative agents,"[2] and that " The increasing power of a growing administrative organization is accentuated by the decreasing power of the rest of the society to resist its further growth and control."[3] To obviate the evils of a powerful bureaucracy it is of the highest importance that regulative policy be held as closely as possible to the lines of least resistance —the lines marked out by natural and economic laws. But it is of equal importance that the regulative policy thus defined be efficiently carried out.

The differentiation of liquor law administration into its

[1] L. F. Ward, *Dynamic Sociology*, II, 573.

[2] Herbert Spencer, *The Coming Slavery*, p. 27.   [3] *Ibid.*, p. 33.

two prime elements, revenue and police, makes possible such a specializing of revenue administration as to add greatly to its efficiency. It is impossible to specialize the police administration of liquor laws with equal completeness; but the experiment of committing the police enforcement of the liquor laws, in a large city, specially to selected officers as well as generally to all, has shown that even the police administration of such laws may be specialized with some degree of definiteness. It would be rash to predict the general employment, at an early day, of experts to guard the peace and moral safety of society, as experts are now employed to examine savings banks and supervise the erection of buildings. It is reasonable to expect, however, that public sentiment generally will compel such a mingling of administrative efficiency with "humanizing" influences in police control as to make it easy for good men everywhere to obey the law, and hard for bad men to evade it. When this standard of administration has been attained, imperfect laws will rectify themselves.

The common view of the problem of enforcement of liquor laws is expressed in the following words which appeared recently in a representative newspaper:

Liquor laws are, we believe, the only laws about which there is much question of construction. When new laws are made as to other things there is frequently dispute as to their meanings; that dispute is settled by a test case, and that is the end of it. But with liquor laws, the construction of which has been settled over and over again, there is this continual wrangling, not really as to the meaning, but, to make a long story short, as to the way in which they should not be enforced. We believe we are waking up to the significance of having a common rule of action enforced so that all people may have protection. Certainly there is now everywhere a strong attempt, and everywhere successful, to enforce liquor laws. . . . It will bring us to the condition that if we do not want the liquor traffic regulated according to the present laws, we will modify those laws. When a people reaches such a stage it has made incalculable advance beyond that in which it is satisfied with having a law and then ignoring it, or " giving it a liberal construction."

This view covers but half the problem of liquor law administration. It is the province of administration not only to secure, by enforcement, the repeal of an untrue expression of the popular will, but, by wise insistence, to conserve the influences that make for social uplift. The administration is the active guardian of the public welfare. In the high degree of differentiation of aims and specialization of functions which political society has attained, the administration must be held responsible for many duties which in former days were left to the voluntary action of private persons; and when accountability to a local constituency does not suffice to secure that conservative activity which makes for public and private well-being, efficiency is in some cases to be sought through the central administration of the commonwealth.

VITA.

THE author of this dissertation, Mr. C. M. Lacey Sites, was born in Foochow, China, October 29, 1865, being the son of the Reverend Nathan Sites, D. D., a missionary of the Methodist Episcopal Church. He came to the United States with his parents at the age of seven years, attended the public schools of Washington, D. C., and was graduated from the Ohio Wesleyan University in 1887 with the degree of A. B. In the same year he was appointed to an instructorship in the Washington high school, three years later became principal of the Capitol Hill high school, and continued in this position until June, 1896. He has accepted an appointment as Professor of Political Science in the Nan-Yang College of Shanghai, China.

During the year 1895–96, he pursued courses in political philosophy in the Columbia University, Washington, under the direction of Professor Lee Davis Lodge and Dr. W. T. Harris. Entering Columbia University as a graduate student in October, 1896, he was appointed to a University Scholarship in political science for the year 1896–97 and to the University Fellowship in constitutional law for the year 1897–98. His major subject was constitutional law combined with comparative administrative law ; his minor subjects were economics and sociology ; he also pursued courses in international law, jurisprudence and political philosophy. He heard lectures by Professors John W. Burgess, Frank J. Goodnow, Richmond Mayo-Smith, Edwin R. A. Seligman, Franklin H. Giddings, John Bassett Moore, Munroe Smith

(163)

and William A. Dunning; and was a member of Professor Burgess's seminar in constitutional law and of Professor Goodnow's seminar in administrative law.

He has received the degree of A. M. (Ohio Wesleyan University, 1890,) and the degree of LL. B. (National Law School, 1890).

www.ingramcontent.com/pod-product-compliance
Lightning Source LLC
Chambersburg PA
CBHW020548270326
41927CB00006B/762